CW01622268

PRAISE FOR *EMPOWERING PEOPLE THROUGH CARING LEADERSHIP*

In my technology recruitment days, I crossed paths with Germain, a standout individual whose inherent goodness left a lasting impression. Despite our paths not aligning professionally, our genuine connection endured over the years. It felt like discovering a hidden gem, and as fate would have it, we reconnected when Germain faced a career detour due to cancer. Entrusted with helping him realign his life's work, I recognized the immense value in collaborating with Germain. Now, as he embarks on writing a book on caring leadership, I'm in awe of the convergence of values and potential. Germain's journey reflects that even in corporate giants, compassionate leaders like him exist. Anticipation builds as Germain unveils his insights. Discovering him and his book is like stumbling upon a buried treasure, a sentiment I plan to cherish and revisit. You'll soon realize that this compassionate individual is truly an inspirational leader.

— Peter Goral, Social Media Strategist, ArtEnvy Inc. (Marketing Solutions)

Empowering People Through Caring Leadership is a beacon for those seeking authentic leadership in a world filled with superficial advice. Germain's approach prioritizes both the well-being of team members and achieving exceptional results, fostering a culture of trust and empowerment. This book is a practical guide for leaders at all levels, offering strategies to navigate today's complex challenges. In a time when compassionate leadership is crucial, Germain's book is a must-read for personal and professional growth.

— Dr. Marshall Goldsmith, Thinkers50 #1 Executive Coach and New York Times bestselling author of *The Earned Life, Triggers, and What Got You Here Won't Get You There*

I've had the privilege of directly observing Germain as an effective, caring leader and how he has inspired so many people who have worked under his leadership. Glad to see that he has reflected on his formula for success and shared it via this book. Very practical, thought-provoking advice, co-mingled with bonus insights from people who have influenced Germain along his journey. For anyone who regards the people in their organization as their greatest asset — this is a must-read guidebook.

— Teresa Short, Vice President, Oracle Consulting

In this wise and practical book filled with insightful examples and stories, Germain St-Denis advises us on how to succeed as Leaders — by living a behavioral conviction toward really caring for our colleagues. The leadership paradigm suggested throughout this text seems so basic, yet when put into context, provides a systematic approach to handling today's real-world challenges.

— Patrick J. McKenna, internationally recognized author, lecturer, strategist and seasoned advisor to the leaders of premier professional service firms

Empowering People Through Caring Leadership by Germain St-Denis is a testament to the power of compassionate leadership and leaders who coach. This book, written with deep insight and sensitivity, is a roadmap to leadership that is not only effective but also empathetic. St-Denis shows us that caring leadership is not a luxury, but a necessity in today's world, where human connection is more important than ever. He empowers us to be leaders who don't just manage but coach, inspire and nurture. This book is a must-read for anyone who aspires to lead from a place of caring and authenticity. St-Denis' wisdom is a beacon for a new era of leadership — one that values people first.

— Rachel Treece, CEO, Henka Institute and author of *The Henka Effect – How Coaching is Transforming Leadership and Organisations*

In *Empowering People Through Caring Leadership,* Germain St-Denis presents a compelling case for the transformative power of compassion in leadership. This book is a treasure trove of insights for anyone who aspires to lead with empathy and genuine concern for their team's well-being and growth. St-Denis weaves practical advice with poignant narratives that illustrate how caring leadership can not only uplift individuals but also drive collective success.

— Dan Hoeyer, Founder and President, Leaders Excellence at Harvard Square

Germain St-Denis is the epitome of a leader who inspires through quiet wisdom. A life in leadership and an outlook shaped by personal challenge and deep self-reflection has produced a master storyteller from whom we can all learn. This book holds such an important message for leaders of today, that the way to impact your people is through Caring Leadership. Germain provides the clear and actionable strategies you need in order to turn wise words into powerful actions that will transform your people and your organization.

— Dr Gary Crotaz, PhD, award-winning author of *The IDEA Mindset* and host of *The Unlock Moment* podcast

Germain St-Denis is one of the rare individuals who cares about people and it comes across loud and clear in his book *Empowering People Through Caring Leadership.* In this book, he explains how results can be achieved in many ways—but primarily how to develop a leadership coaching style that grows the organization through nurturing the growth of the people you lead. Read this book as it will help you learn how to lean into a more natural approach to leadership — empowering people by caring for them.

— Joe Murphy, Vice President Employer Services, Maximus

Germain's book brings a unique holistic and collaborative insight that transcends stereotypes. I find it a practical "From People to People Leadership" roadmap with real-world examples that vividly illustrate the principles of authentic and people-centric leadership rooted in human values, engagement and empowerment. Simplifying leadership in its application is what makes it most precious to aspiring and confirmed leaders. I appreciate how the book specifically highlights the strength of women through its people-caring culture and Coaching Leadership style. This makes it a precious read for women aspiring to lead authentically and excel in their unapologetic journey of impactful excellence.

— Saliha Oukaci, The Impression Architect, Executive Leadership Presence for Women

Theodore Roosevelt famously said, "People don't care how much you know until they know how much you care." I can't think of a better quote that encapsulates the profound leadership strategies by author Germain St-Denis in his new book, *Empowering People Through Caring Leadership.* Caring leadership impacts performance, retention, and the quality of life of the human beings you serve, and if you're looking to take your leadership development to a heartfelt level, this book is a perfect guide to help get you there!

— Harry Flaris, Founder and CEO, Inspiration with Flair Consulting Services

Germain St-Denis takes on a bold and challenging approach to leadership by flipping some of the conventional paradigms on their head. During our interactions over the years, he has always held a "people as people first" view of leadership. Germain isn't just an author who has developed a catchy concept; rather, he writes from a place of deep conviction and proven results. The strategies Germain describes require personal growth and daily discipline, so that someone can create a leadership platform that is not based on personal achievement, rather, it is based on the impact the leader has on others.

— Doug Dawson, author and leadership consultant

A must-read that brilliantly captures the essence of what it takes to be a great Caring Leader and the tremendous opportunities this creates. It's an invaluable resource for leaders who aspire to unlock the best in their people and for caring leaders seeking affirmation that they're on the right path. St-Denis illustrates that leaders who are sometimes even labeled as over caring are in fact the catalysts driving their teams to exceptional heights of performance and engagement, resulting in truly remarkable outcomes.

— Lucie Maillet St-Pierre, former VP Customer Success Salesforce, Central Europe, Advisory. Board Member Women in Tech Switzerland - engaging on DE&I and Sustainability programs

EMPOWERING PEOPLE THROUGH CARING LEADERSHIP

STRATEGIES THAT *ACTUALLY* WORK!

GERMAIN L. ST-DENIS

Live Life **Happy**
Publishing

Published and Distributed in Canada by Live Life Happy Publishing.
www.livelifehappypublishing.com

Library of Congress Cataloging-in-Publication Data

St-Denis, Germain L.

Empowering People Through Caring Leadership: Strategies That *Actually* Work!

Categories:

Books › Business Leadership

Books › Business Mentoring & Coaching

Books › Professional & Technical Management

Paper Back Book ISBN: 978-1-990461-66-8

E-Book ISBN: 978-1-990461-67-5

Cover Design: Germain L. St-Denis

Live Life Happy Publishing

PUBLISHER'S NOTE & AUTHOR DISCLAIMER

Dedicated to those leaders who strive to create a better, more caring workplace for those who work with them. To lead is a privilege, not a right. Be kind.

« Je ne trempe pas ma plume dans
l'encrier mais dans la vie. »

"I do not dip my pen in the inkwell,
but into life."

— Blaise Cendrars
French poet and novelist

FOREWORD

By Mark C. Crowley, author of *Lead From The Heart*

Dear Readers,

The author of the book you're about to read is authentically caring, thoughtful and generous. I point this out because many books on leadership have been written by people who don't "walk the talk" or fully embody the lessons they teach.

I first met Germain St-Denis via our interactions on social media where he routinely demonstrated a passionate commitment to caring, compassionate and people-centred leadership. Over and over, what has stood out about Germain is his natural inclination to compliment, promote and otherwise support the work of other authors – work and ideas he admires and therefore chooses to spotlight. In a world where people often compete with one another for attention, Germain stands apart by embracing an abundance mindset and by choosing to honour his peers knowing it will only enhance his own work.

I am a grateful recipient of Germain's munificence – in fact, his book embodies many of my *Lead From The Heart* principles. But as you'll read, he also takes readers through his own journey as a caring leader and as an advocate for servant leadership and people first principles.

And so, I am thrilled to introduce you to Germain's new book, *Empowering People Through Caring Leadership: Strategies That Actually Work*. In it, he introduces his Architect of People First™ approach, which captures the essence of his leadership style, beliefs and principles. It lays out the foundation for caring leadership, where leaders prioritize the well-being, growth and development of their team members while concurrently pursuing their most important goals.

As you'll read, Germain believes that that heart of leadership is human connection. This leadership philosophy places people at the centre of decision-making in a world where leaders act as coaches, mentors and advocates for their team members. It's a leadership thesis that not only drives results but also fosters a culture of trust, teamwork, collaboration, accountability and empowerment.

This book is not about theories or abstract concepts; it is a practical guide for aspiring, new and experienced leaders to lead more effectively. Having led teams through crises, acquisitions, recessions and executive churn, Germain offers proven strategies to help you navigate our complex and unpredictable world and its challenges.

At a time when people desperately need *caring* leaders, leaders with a *heart*, I'm certain you'll find Germain's book tremendously rewarding, both personally and professionally.

MCC

INTRODUCTION

"Even the smallest act of caring for another person is like a drop of water; it will make ripples throughout the entire pond."

— Jessy and Bryan Matteo

Not another book of Leadership BS — who cares? I care and I am convinced that when leaders care, people care and great things can happen!

How did I end up becoming an advocate of Servant Leadership, People First and Caring Leadership principles, and subsequently formulating my Architect of People First™ strategies? Read on!

Early Days

You may wonder why an average guy from rural Ontario who studied and worked in emerging technology and management consulting services would write a book on leadership. Growing up on a farm in a large, kind-hearted family, I observed and admired my parents' tenacity and determination whenever they faced adversity. Through both favourable and tough times, their patient, loving care for us never faltered. And while my lifelong health issues began at a young age, my parents' example taught me to never let difficult challenges prevent me from doing my best to achieve all that I set my heart on. I knew that like them, I, too, could be resilient and caring and successful.

My career has been a typical one, starting as a software developer before becoming a tech lead, then architect, strategist and thought leader on various emerging technologies and related professional services. Through my career progression, I became increasingly interested in business applications and the impact that the adoption of these rapid innovations had on the people concerned. I observed first-hand how leadership styles and personalities affected people tremendously, both professionally and personally.

I worked with excellent leaders and leadership teams. However, I also experienced lousy leaders, micromanagers and arrogant bully leaders. They left people feeling depressed and discouraged because they didn't care about their staff, didn't trust them, focused only on money, or were simply incompetent in their leadership role. These leaders created toxic, demoralizing environments instead of rich, rewarding experiences where people and organizations could flourish. Unfortunately, examples of poor leadership and challenging cultures seemed similarly prevalent and damaging in many other fields and industries, not only technology or consulting services.

Core family values such as caring, empathy, trust, teamwork, determination and resilience have undoubtedly guided me through life as an adult. This influence is likely why I became a huge advocate of Servant Leadership and People First principles over time, initially not realizing that this leadership style was helping me all along. Leaders who fail to realize that people are primarily driven by emotions miss the mark completely.

While *servant leadership* is a timeless concept, the term as it relates to leadership style was coined by Robert K. Greenleaf in "The Servant as Leader", an essay that he first published in 1970. In it Greenleaf said, "The servant-leader is servant first... It begins with the natural feeling that one wants to serve, to serve first."

Leadership experts and renowned authors such as John Maxwell and Ken Blanchard wholeheartedly embrace Servant Leadership. Servant Leaders care about people and focus on providing a more humane experience for everyone.

"You can employ [people] and hire hands to work for you, but you must win their hearts to have them work with you."

— Merle Shain, Canadian author and journalist

Architect of People First™ on a Mission

In 2015, after a routine hip replacement that I'd like to think made me more "hip", I was diagnosed with and subsequently successfully treated for a malignant tumour on a vocal cord. Rather than returning to work, my wife and I resigned from our corporate jobs, took a break, travelled and enjoyed spending time in nature, which is always regenerative. However, over time, I began to miss work, the people and the leadership experience.

Since I had developed many strong relationships, I kept in touch with several former colleagues and team members. I followed developments in the workplace along with the latest trends. I started to write on social media to share and refine my thinking about Caring Leadership and employee empowerment. This activity created a following that led to podcast invitations to discuss my ideas. In 2019, I created my Architect of People First™ approach which includes strategies for Caring Leadership that I know really work.

Today, my mission is to share my Caring Leadership principles to help develop better leaders and empower them and their teams, thus creating a better workplace culture for everyone. That is the motivation behind this book. People desperately need Caring Leaders who will coach them in their career growth and support them in challenging circumstances.

In a period of tremendous change and uncertainty, shaping an effective workplace culture is a critical task for C-suite executive leaders. By adopting Architect of People First™ strategies and Caring Leadership principles, senior leadership teams can further develop and enhance the capabilities of their leaders and managers. Leaders who inspire and empower those around them unlock their team's potential and achieve tremendous success together.

I want others to benefit from my experience as a former director, senior director and vice-president leading high-performing, loyal teams with diverse skill sets across a vast geography, and helping commercial and public sector clients with a wide variety of technologies and business applications.

I share real-life stories, successes and challenges along the way that reflect the tremendous benefits of this leadership philosophy and mindset. I selected a limited number of significant topics that focus on critical areas that impact workers and leaders today and in the foreseeable future. These include:

1. Caring Leadership and coaching

2. Motivating and developing people

3. Leading multigenerational teams

4. Nurturing the human connection and work relationships while embracing the Future of Work

5. Dealing with life's challenges — the tough stuff

I hope you, dear reader — an aspiring, new or experienced leader — find these topics and stories inspiring.

"You will never be a leader that others love to follow if you are not a leader that loves people."

— Steve Gutzler, author and motivational speaker

A Bonus and a Promise

Throughout my book, I also include insights that I solicited from other leaders, renowned authors, leadership experts and former colleagues and staff. I am incredibly grateful to all who graciously shared their experiences, observations and wisdom. All of these individuals have shown unequivocal support for Caring Leadership and a people-focused culture. I find it highly encouraging, and I believe that together, we *can* create a better workplace for everyone!

As you read each chapter, I hope your commitment to the benefits of caring about people and of trusting and empowering them deepens. You may already sense the tremendous energy and potential that this leadership philosophy holds for you and your people.

"The most important thing in good leadership is truly caring. The best leaders in any profession care about the people they lead, and the people who are being led know when the caring is genuine and when it's faked or not there at all."

— *Twelve Leadership Principles of Dean Smith* by David Chadwick, former basketball player

PART ONE:

What is Caring Leadership and Why is it Important?

CHAPTER 1

Foundations of Caring Leadership and Architect of People First™

"I used to think that if you cared for other people, you need to study sociology or something like it. But... I [have] concluded, if you want to help other people, be a manager. Management is the most noble of professions if it's practiced well. No other occupation offers as many ways to help others learn and grow, take responsibility and be recognized for achievement, and contribute to the success of a team."

— Clayton Christensen, Harvard Business School professor and bestselling author

A Moment in Time

In the '90s, I worked for a top-rated Canadian IT services firm in Ottawa, Ontario — experts in technology development, program delivery and management consulting. A short time after joining, I fell ill. I felt terrible about the situation. Although I had performed well in my job, I had delivered only a few projects and was worried about the company's reaction to my being ill. However, everything was fine. Everyone was very supportive, cared for my well-being and gave me time to recover. The senior consultant who initially interviewed me was my mentor. He was terrific, really understanding — he cared. You can appreciate that this helped me focus on getting better rather than worrying about job security. His support signified a great culture where leaders cared about people. I would recall this at a critical time later in my career. By the way, this mentor and I still connect occasionally, even though we worked together 30 years ago.

Once I recovered, I was in full form. Because of my background and experience with various clients and emerging technological developments, I was assigned to exciting leading-edge projects. I loved it and I worked hard as a "road warrior", travelling extensively to clients and engaging with them at various organizational levels. My boss, our management consulting practice leader, gave me lots of autonomy and freedom. I felt supported, trusted and empowered.

Some time later, I landed a local engagement and enjoyed being around fellow consultants and members of the leadership team. One day, a surprise announcement came: the leadership team appointed me head of the management consulting practice. I was floored — what an honour! But I thought, why me? Why did they choose me over a few others in the group who I felt were equally qualified and perhaps even stronger candidates? That took a long time to sink in. I wondered how these people would react to this major change. My mentor had moved on by then; otherwise, he may have been the one to lead the group.

Here's a key takeaway that will resonate throughout this book: **Caring Leadership, trust, empowerment and recognition inspire people to perform at their best.**

Assuming the Lead Role

As I moved into my new leadership role, I remembered how the staff, consultants and management team had been so good to me. I knew many of them well enough to understand how extremely competent my team members were – the bar was high. I needed their support to have any chance of succeeding. I also needed to care for them and help them grow. It was at this point that I started to consciously conceptualize what a leadership role like this should be. It should be to help people be their best. That's how I set my mantra as a leader: **Be a Caring Leader and help people to be their best.**

Where to begin? I quickly organized a practice meeting as an informal "meet and greet" pizza lunch for everyone who could attend. I wanted an opportunity to get to know all the team members, both professionally and personally. One-on-one meetings followed. To better understand our practice and all our management consulting services, I formed a working group consisting of senior associates. Everyone was very willing to pitch in. We met regularly and discussed a range of key topics, including primary services, client expectations, developing trends, engagement strategies, what works and what doesn't, career development, etc. Doing this gave them a voice and it was a great learning experience for all of us.

The cooperation and support I received from everyone in the group and the leadership team were superb. The entire practice was energized and our group delivered excellent results. We liked to have fun, exchanged jokes and quotes, and always enjoyed frank, open dialogue. That was one of the best periods of my career and for many others, too. Until we were acquired.

As a side note, I wish I had Patrick McKenna's book *First Among Equals* to guide me at the time. Its title alone perfectly reflects the situation that I found myself in. Patrick writes, "To succeed in your leadership role, you will also need a special set of skills: the ability to influence other people's emotions, feelings, attitudes and their determination."

Looking back at my earlier leadership roles, I didn't spend much time thinking about my leadership style. It was likely because I was exceptionally busy as a leading expert, strategist and thought leader. At one point, I was in a leading role internationally, which added a whole new dimension to my evolving career. Over time, I was trusted with larger teams and more senior roles. As a leader of leaders and managers, I had to deal with highly challenging circumstances such as recessions and acquisitions, at times with not very caring bosses and in toxic cultures. These experiences brought Caring Leadership to the forefront of my thinking. I have maintained my Caring Leadership philosophy in all my subsequent leadership roles and still rely on it today in my coaching and consulting work.

In this book, I share some true stories, experiences and relationships that reflect the tremendous benefits of Caring Leadership and putting People First. I hope you find these inspiring and that they help you through both good and uncertain times.

Fast Forward to 2023

In spring 2023, I was honoured to be invited as a guest on *The Unlock Moment* podcast with Dr Gary Crotaz, PhD, an accomplished global thought leader and executive coach in the UK. He wanted to unpack my understanding of Servant Leadership and Caring Leadership. His questions were very well thought out. At one point during the conversation Gary said, "I love the simplicity of your articulation of servant leadership: train and equip your people, and then trust and empower them."

Yes, Caring Leadership is that simple. In our rapidly changing and uncertain times, people desperately need caring leaders. However, it is not easy for everyone. Many leaders don't get it. It is difficult for them to trust and empower others. Some actually compete with their staff. Why? Do they fear losing authority and power? Do they feel superior and believe that they must constantly tell people how to do their job? Do they think people will only work if they look over their shoulder?

Renowned leadership expert John Maxwell says only secure leaders give power to others. They spend their time identifying leaders, building them up, giving them resources, authority and responsibility, and then turning them loose to achieve.

Caring Leadership is helping people to be their best. You will read this statement several times in this book, possibly memorize it or even tattoo it in your brain as I have in mine!

What are the Hallmarks of Caring Leadership?

1. Care about people, recognizing that we are all complex and imperfect – warts and all.

2. Develop strong, trusting relationships: make it personal.

3. Understand the role of individual values and how they drive our feelings and behaviours.

4. Get to know your team as individuals: understand their aspirations, concerns and what motivates them.

5. Be a Servant Leader — anyone who is not ready to serve should not be a leader.

6. Embody the principles of respect, trust, authenticity, integrity, humility, teamwork and resilience.

7. Be available, be present, be intentional in all interactions, be an empathetic listener.

8. Put People First: consider how changes, decisions, tasks, demands and even your tone impact people and their well-being.

9. Develop and leverage individual and team strengths.

10. Treat people as partners, each making a key contribution to your team's and your organization's success, as well as their own personal success.

> "Success as a leader requires effort.
> Get to know your team as people first,
> understand their potential as professionals,
> then trust and empower them to get the job done."
>
> — Germain St-Denis

How Do We Measure Success Under Caring Leadership?

Simply put, success is observed in the people and team(s) you lead. They will become engaged, motivated and able to achieve specific goals and results, both personal and corporate. They will grow and perform in ways they only could have with your leadership and guidance.

To some, this sounds too generic and soft. However, a key differentiator is that people are happy to work with you and enjoy the journey. They don't dread Monday mornings, and they are not worried when you ask to talk to them. Instead, they look forward to seeing you.

I can assure you that Caring Leadership works. I've been blessed to work with terrific people who performed well in all kinds of demanding circumstances and remained loyal. I truly appreciate the solid and lasting relationships we developed. I'm still in touch with people I worked with 30 years ago and three years ago.

That's not the case everywhere, of course. The 2022 McKinsey survey "Why are people leaving the workforce?" found that uncaring leaders ranks among the top three reasons people leave a company or don't join a new one.

Enter Architect of People First™

Architect of People First™ captures the essence of my leadership style, beliefs and principles. It is based on years of experience and a demonstrated history of creating and leading high-performing, loyal teams who consistently delivered solid results. It's about human values, engagement and empowerment, and aligns with established paradigms such as Servant Leadership, People First, and Leading from The Heart.

Architect of People First™ is my branded strategic approach to becoming a successful Caring Leader and achieving the right mindset that goes with it. These are strategies that you and others can emulate and benefit from. Here are the core elements of my approach:

1. Be a kind, caring person and a Coaching Leader.

2. Develop trusting relationships and understand what motivates people.

3. Master the art of working with multigenerational, multifunctional and multicultural teams.

4. Get through the "tough stuff" by drawing on your experience and the experience of others.

5. Evolve with and influence the Future of Work, be flexible, adaptable and open-minded.

Self-Reflection Question: Are You Ready to Put People First, to Be a Caring Leader?

Architect of People First™ and Caring Leadership are part of my brand. They are on my website and are headlines and taglines on my social media platforms. But they're not slogans. It's all about *mindset*!

Being a Caring Leader or Servant Leader is not rocket science, although the study of human behaviour and neuroscience is most interesting and genuinely insightful. We are all human beings. When leaders care, people care! Ken Blanchard, renowned author and leadership expert, writes in his book *Simple Truths* that Servant Leadership is the best way to achieve both great results and great relationships.

Even in the most challenging situations, caring and listening with empathy and compassion can make an enormous difference. Letting someone go is the most difficult of a manager's responsibilities. I dreaded it each time, and I did it as humanely as I could. That's the least one can do. I remember having to demote a manager once because the person's reputation was badly tarnished. I was new and didn't see that, but the move was necessary to change the dynamics of the organization. Another time, I was asked to let staff go because we didn't have enough work. All my people were strong performers. I pushed back, but to no avail. The executive office mandated at least one headcount reduction in each region. I had to choose one team member. The person was shocked. I started by apologizing and I concluded by apologizing. This aspect of leadership is never easy. I'm grateful that these fine people did not hold it against me. Some have even stayed in touch.

Why Should You Read This Book?

Being a Caring Leader, applying principles of Servant Leadership and People First comes naturally to me. I'm a people person, an upbeat, curious and fun-loving kinda guy – that is a blessing. I understand that's not the case for everyone, and I want to help everyone, including those less naturally inclined. That includes you!

I want to help aspiring, new and experienced leaders of every stripe create a Caring Leadership workplace culture so that they and their teams can be their absolute best and thrive. My Architect of People First™ proven strategies can guide you along the way. After reading this book, I hope you'll understand the value of putting People First and can apply principles of empowerment through Caring Leadership in your leadership journey.

I like to use various real-life scenarios I've experienced to help you, my readers, understand how being a Caring Leader is such a winning leadership style for everyone. People who worked with me in the past may relate to specific situations and examples I share in this book. I am truly thankful that we were part of each other's journey.

You, too, can obtain the highest level of cooperation, loyalty, engagement and performance from people, simply because in a Caring Leadership and People First culture they're happy to do so. There is no better way!

BONUS INSIGHTS

Leader Bonus Insight

My most memorable experience was when my entire team was stressed and flailing, and one of my customers asked to have me removed as project manager because I had lost all credibility in missing another delivery date. I sat down with my Boss/Mentor, and rather than be angry with me or remind me how bad things were, he reminded me of the reasons I was so good. A lecture on why he thought I was Great. The amount of energy that I received from that conversation helped me remove all obstacles. I felt that I had found my super cape when I left the room.

— Teresa Short, Vice President, Oracle Consulting Services

Leader Bonus Insight

I believe that if you are authentic and you truly care about your team, they know; they feel it. They trust you; they know they have your support, and it creates an environment where people are free to share challenges, and this helps the team pull together to solve them. My advice will always be to be yourself. When you try to act the way you think you "should" people see through it, and it can be truly damaging to the culture of the team. Help your team grow and develop or enhance skills. The fastest way to show you care is to invest in their future.

—A humble leader and former leadership colleague

Team Member Bonus Insight

I strongly believe that a good manager, and this applies to any employee, needs to have the right balance between the human aspect and the work aspect. On the human aspect, my manager always put the person in front of any other urgency. This is a rare quality in a world where we are mostly being asked to deliver at any cost. But we are humans. I don't believe that you can get the best of a person by screaming or by pushing on late nights without knowing the person first. My manager always wanted to know the person first, making sure he/she is always in a comfort zone first, and ready for the challenge. Then my manager can motivate each individual to achieve because he has gained the trust of the person, he will always get the best of him/her. On the work aspect, for the time we have been working together, my manager's ability to balance his time between people management and business management was remarkable. I was one of his remote direct reports, but the distance did not lessen his presence in the team. He successfully built a strong hybrid/remote team. Every time I needed him, he was always available, he was always able to find time to help regardless of what I needed help for. Sometimes to prepare a presentation, sometimes to prepare a meeting, sometimes to overcome obstacles that I judged too hard to overcome on my own.

— Max Pellizzaro, Principal Technical Project Manager, Amazon

Team Member and Leader Bonus Insight

My specific memory is of a leader, before a major presentation to a client, who looked at me and said, "I'm going for a walk - you do the briefing". So, I did, not without trepidation. Afterwards, my senior told me "You'd done the analysis and led putting the briefing together. I knew you could do it if you had to. So, I made you." And it worked - big confidence builder.

— Paul Butler, Management Consultant, former Director and General Manager

CHAPTER 2

Leadership Styles and Responsibilities

"Leadership is providing inspiration and vision, then developing and empowering others to achieve this vision."

— Marshall Goldsmith, bestselling author, executive educator and coach

I'm the boss — do what I tell you to do. Nope! That is very different from how good leadership works in today's workplace. If you have a big ego and are looking for the title, glory and money, you are sorely mistaken. However, if you are committed and want to learn how to be a great leader, this book and the information in it may help you. To be a leader, you must understand and be ready to assume the responsibilities of leadership, responsibilities that come with authority and power. Here is the generally accepted Golden Rule of Leadership: **Leadership is a privilege, not a right. When you're in a leadership role, your influence may affect the trajectories of people's entire career and often their lives.** In other words... DON'T SCREW UP OTHER PEOPLE'S LIVES!

What's in it for Me as a Caring Leader, You Ask?

To be happy as a Caring Leader, you must be prepared to obtain job satisfaction and fulfillment through other people's success — the success of your teams and your organization depend on it. It takes work and may require a lot of extra effort. Yet, it is gratifying to see people succeed, knowing you had a role to play in making that happen. As *Lead from The Heart* author Mark Crowley says, "If you don't have an inclination to care about the success and well-being of other people, you shouldn't be managing people."

What Type of Leader Are You?

To understand leadership, it's essential to look at leadership styles and Emotional Intelligence. In his book *Primal Leadership – Realizing the Power of Emotional Intelligence* Daniel Goleman writes, "At its root, then, the primal job of leadership is emotional… Without a healthy dose of heart, a supposed leader may manage, but he does not lead." Goleman says that when a leader creates resonance, you can read it in people's eyes: they're engaged, and they light up. The glue that holds a team together and that commits people to an organization is the emotion they feel.

I first read *Primal Leadership* over 20 years ago and still find it an excellent reference in today's changing world. It will help you understand Emotional Intelligence and it covers the main leadership styles in some detail. Based on extensive research, Goleman says that four of these styles — visionary, coaching, affiliative and democratic – create the kind of resonance that boosts performance, while the remaining two – pacesetting and commanding – although useful in some very specific situations, should be applied with caution. I wholeheartedly agree with Goleman that by teaching people to tune in to their emotions with intelligence and to expand their circles of caring, we can transform organizations from the inside out and make a positive difference in our world.

A leader's style impacts how people respond. We all tend to have a preference or natural approach to leadership. Leadership styles often develop from factors influenced by our personality, upbringing, learning, experiences and role models. It may be appropriate to draw on the other styles depending on the situation to ensure that you are truly effective. It's important to note that emotionally intelligent leaders adapt their leadership style to different situations or the group they lead. By relating to their people on an emotional level, these leaders even switch between leadership styles. The key is to use the right style at the right time – not always easy.

Of course, you don't need to be an Emotional Intelligence expert to understand the role emotions play in people and leadership. I'm simplifying, but you get it: Caring Leadership and a People First culture yield maximum engagement, loyalty and performance.

Consider these two opposite scenarios. An employee makes a mistake, potentially impacting a client. A more senior employee urgently steps in to rectify the problem. Praise that senior person and the team-oriented culture. The manager and the employee then have a coaching discussion. A different leader's reaction might be, "I'm a VP, and I have the power to fire that person."

Coaching affiliative style versus commanding authoritative style – which would you prefer as your boss' style?

We know from experience and the past 3-4 years with the pandemic-imposed restrictions and rapid workplace evolution that caring, understanding, empathy and compassion are essential leadership skills. A people-centric culture and Coaching Leadership style is often best suited to leveraging individual and group strengths. This style is also best for multigenerational and multicultural teams. We'll explore success strategies for the Coaching Leader in more depth in Chapter 3.

Caring Leadership Behind the Scenes

Regardless of style, leadership is a big responsibility: people leadership, team building, career development, coaching and mentoring – all while solving problems and achieving goals set by the organization. A Caring Leader develops and empowers people while getting the job done. Such a leader also develops and empowers other leaders. Peter Drucker, author and management guru, puts it succinctly, "Rank does not confer privilege or give power. It imposes responsibility."

Our expectations and perceptions of leadership are often deeply misunderstood. Working to be a good or great leader is much more challenging than many people realize. Having never been in a leadership position, most employees will never know how often Caring Leaders work for them and champion them behind the scenes. I can tell you from experience that leaders must fight for their people in the background, often and hard. Yet the team can reap the benefits. You're undoubtedly familiar with these employee scenarios, but do you realize what is done by some leaders in the background?

- A team member does a good job, receives praise, or obtains a new certification, yet these accomplishments may go unnoticed. You acknowledge, appreciate and quietly pass some or all of this on as feedback to upper management and peers. These actions give the individual visibility while demonstrating the development of a strong team. Higher management will appreciate both aspects. Tell the individual you value them and that you shared their achievements with your boss. They'll be thrilled and motivated. When the time comes for opportunities to take on key projects, new roles, promotions or bonuses, the individual(s) that the leader puts forward will already be known, even if just slightly, to upper management and will potentially be better received in the process.

- One of your "road warriors" has travelled extensively and worked a significant amount of extra (unpaid) hours to meet the demands of a key client and ensure the successful implementation and deployment of a critical application. You provide detailed justification for this worker to receive an additional amount when incentive bonuses are paid.

Servant Leadership - To Be a Leader, You Must Be Ready to Serve

There's an excellent video, *Servant Leadership — A Minute with John Maxwell*, on YouTube. Here's what he says: "Servant

Leaders have the most loyal people around them because people see beyond their leadership skills. They see their heart. When you have good leadership skills and you have it complemented with a great heart to add value to people, that's where you get the loyalty of your people in your team. You're the kind of person they'll work for and die for because they know you would do the same for them."

Debunking the Myth

You may have heard some people say that Servant Leaders and Caring Leaders are soft and people can get away with less effort — *not so*! Caring Leadership does not mean people can slack off and get away with it. Work needs to get done. The team's and the organization's goals must be met. Expectations remain high and everyone is accountable.

> *"Leaders become great, not because of their power, but because of their ability to empower others."*
>
> — John C. Maxwell, author and leadership guru

BONUS INSIGHTS

Leader Bonus Insight

I've benefited from so many wonderful leaders and mentors. But I think I am going to have to talk about Ron Oberlander, former CEO of Canadian paper giant Abitibi-Price. Ron brought together three things that I believe drove performance in others: he lived it first, he looked for potential, he had vulnerable strength. He talked about the values of the company constantly and why they mattered, but he also showed how they mattered. Second, he looked for potential. I'll never forget him showing me a job posting in our office one day that had a 5-7 years in role requirement. "Michael, if we find a person stuck only doing that job for that long then we do NOT want them, they're going nowhere. We hire for the potential, the ability to do a job, then let people learn that job, grow in it, and move on." And finally, his vulnerability and strength. He made it crystal clear that anyone could challenge him. Rank did not make you infallible. And he didn't just roll over, he'd engage in the contest with vigor, but never with power. He kept that out of it and it was all about reasoning and thinking it through. Oftentimes the other party would come around to his way of thinking, but there were plenty of times he changed his mind and then he always did two things: thank that person publicly and tell others he had changed his mind and why. He celebrated being educated. It was the example he set and the way I wanted to be like him that caused me to perform.

—Michael Leckie, Founding Partner, Silverback Partners

Colleague and Leader Bonus Insight

There is always room in an organization for more talented people. The more talent in the organization the better because as the organization succeeds it provides greater opportunities for everyone. Too many leaders view talented people as a threat to their own power as these people begin to move up the ladder. Such leaders are more concerned about their personal success than they are about the collective success of the organization. I love being the dumbest person in the room because it provides the best opportunity to learn. Leaders who insist on behaving as though they are the smartest person in the room don't learn and develop themselves and don't provide others with the opportunity to learn and develop.

—Evan Diamond, Management Consultant and former Vice President, Fujitsu Consulting

Team Member Bonus Insight

My mentor is my biggest fan. He believes in me, trusts me and respects my opinion.

—Sylvie Dubois, Senior Business Analyst, Government of Canada

PART TWO:

The How of Caring Leadership (A Collaborative Coaching Approach)

CHAPTER 3

The Caring Leader as a Coach

"Successful people become great leaders when they learn to shift the focus from themselves to others."

— Marshall Goldsmith, renowned leadership expert and top executive coach

Do you remember your first boss? What was the person like? Did this person influence your skills development and career path?

For my first job, I was thrilled to join a telco's computer communications group, a happening place back then. My manager was a tall, soft-spoken and kind-hearted man named Warren. I had so much to learn, both technically and professionally. I was learning how to work: how work gets assigned, completed, reviewed and approved. Warren was terrific at explaining the process, mentoring and coaching us along. We could see he cared. Our technical lead, Pat, was bright, full of energy and ambition. He challenged us technically and in our drive to learn and achieve. He did so in a cheerful, easy manner (a description that a boss applied to me years later) that encouraged and motivated us. Our group performed well, and under Warren and Pat's steady, encouraging guidance, I performed beyond my expectations in my first few years. Looking back decades later, I can see now that they were both excellent leaders, mentors, coaches and role models for me. Caring, motivating leadership translated into great results. The organizational model worked.

Or did it? A parallel team was under a manager, Mr X, with its own tech lead. In the other group, we'd hear complaints about Mr X needing to be kinder to his team. He did not have the same leadership style as my boss, which made a huge difference to people's employee experience in that group. Based on my observation of our two teams, I concluded that the organizational model worked with the right person and the right leadership style.

The best leaders are not necessarily experts in their field. Instead, they call on experts to work with their team. I've used this model many times in my career as a strategist, program director and in leadership roles. So often what happens is that people who excel as individual contributors are promoted into leadership roles, yet some are simply not people leaders. I've always considered this a severe flaw in the modern workplace. We need parallel paths for people leaders and non-people leaders. Several renowned authors, leaders and influencers support this view. It's a tough challenge and a topic we will leave for another day.

Coaching: Let's Talk About Sports

In pro tennis, it's mainly about the individual. Coaches are often past pros bringing technical expertise, on-court experience and emotional support in stressful times. In team sports such as hockey, baseball and soccer, it's mainly about the team. There, the coach is more of a game strategist, a cheerleader and a Coaching Leader, leveraging both individual and team strengths. The value of a Coaching Leader doesn't just lie in their knowledge, experience and skills, but in their ability to impart these effectively and inspire their people.

Is a business leader a coach? Many well-known, influential people and organizations favour leaders as coaches.

- Garry Ridge, former CEO, WD-40 Company: "Your role as a leader is to be the best possible coach you can be for the people that you're privileged to lead."

- Tom Ziglar, motivational speaker: "Coach leaders choreograph the dance between autonomy and authority."

- Ken Blanchard, Servant Leadership guru: "In the past, a leader was a boss. Today's leaders must be partners with their people. They no longer can lead solely based on positional power."

- Marshall Goldsmith, world's leading executive coach: "Coaching is far more effective than training and development."

- Mark Crowley, author and leadership consultant: "I've long believed that all workplace managers should have a coach."

Note that last point: not only should managers be coaches to employees, all workplace leaders should have coaches. There are considerable benefits to having coaches or mentors from both inside and outside the organization. They bring very different perspectives. The best periods of my career have been when I had someone I could count on and reach out to. It pays to bounce your ideas off someone else, ask questions and listen.

How Does Coaching Leadership Work in Practice?

Before jumping in and trying to coach everyone on day one, leaders should get to know the individuals, observe the team dynamics, and understand the corporate culture. Establish trust and build relationships first. Being kind, caring and genuine builds trust. Strong relationships built around trust and accountability make every coaching experience more effective and enjoyable.

C.O.A.C.H. – A Coaching Leader model

Check out this infographic I created based on Patrick J. McKenna's new C.O.A.C.H. model. Patrick is an internationally recognized author and strategist. Thank you so much, Patrick, for sharing this nugget of wisdom.

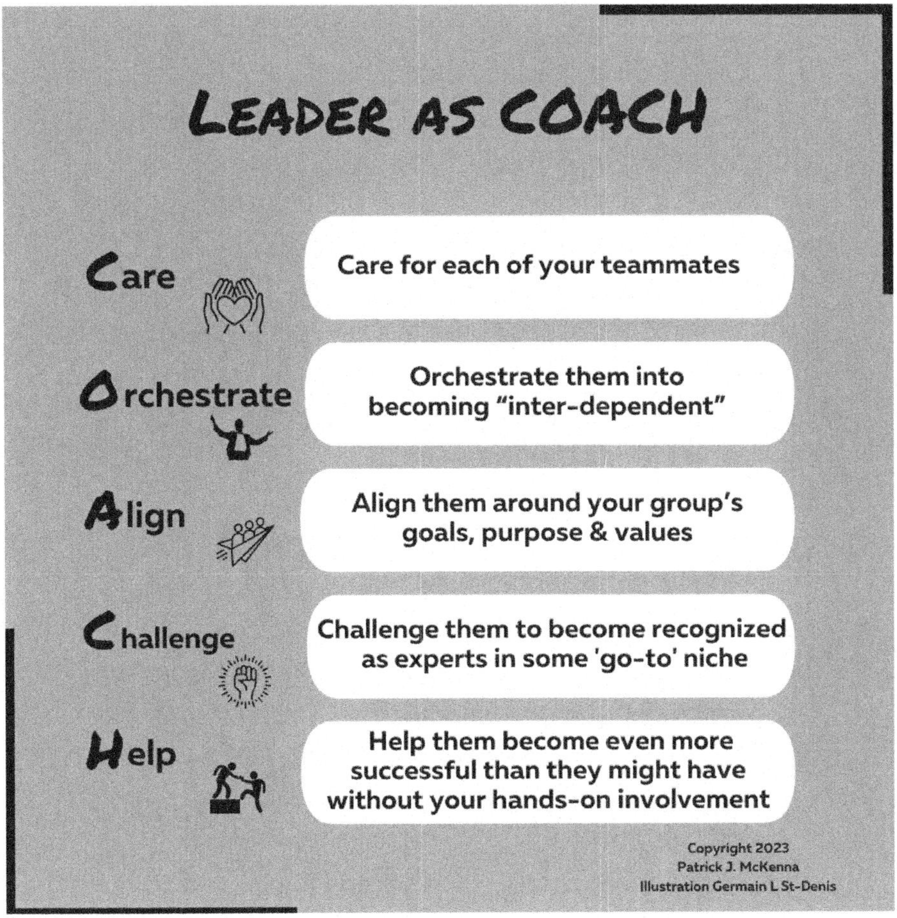

If you're wondering about the illustration, I tried a few generative AI defined images but discounted them. I then decided to create my own infographic using Canva®. Just like this book, it is my own creation.

There is tremendous wisdom in this C.O.A.C.H. model. When I look at it relative to my experience leading, coaching and mentoring teams, I can see close alignment with my Architect of People First™ and Caring Leadership strategies.

Your job as a Coaching Leader:

1. *Get to know your team, one by one.* Find out about them as individuals, what makes them tick, their concerns, ambitions, etc. Make a personal connection, not just a work connection. Show that you care.

2. Bring people together. Brainstorm together to strategize, innovate and solve problems. It's a great way to develop and strengthen relationships, to give people a sense of belonging and community, and a chance to grow. We all need it. Teamwork makes dreamwork!

3. Ensure employees know how their contribution helps the organization meet its goals as they work towards their individual goals; it's a win-win perspective. Better still, tell employees that you, leaders and the company value them and their contribution. Recognition goes a long way. Too many leaders miss this.

4. Understand what motivates or holds back everyone in the organization. Help them overcome their fears and challenges. Allow them the opportunity to tackle something new or unique. Help them shine by leveraging their unique strengths and by showcasing their accomplishments. This works wonders.

5. *Help uncover and release each team member's full potential.* When you get to know people, including the quiet introvert types, you often discover hidden strengths that you can leverage to help the person succeed while

they help the team and organization. This must be one of the most underrated and underutilized areas of leadership. There are gold mines of untapped potential out there.

A quick real-life story

As she made significant organizational changes, my boss called me one morning to say that a particular group of functional resources were being added to my technical team. Oh? Ok. I knew what I had to do. I had previously met a couple of these people briefly. I called all 23 of them individually for a quick introduction and check-in. A week or two later, my boss told me, "People like reporting to you because you ask about them as a person."

In the above situation, it was of utmost importance to reach out quickly, acknowledge each person, and set the foundation for a solid relationship. We will delve into this in Chapter 4.

"Members of your team will profit when you learn to promote understanding, provide them with adequate knowledge, facilitate effective interaction, and conduct effective meetings."

— Phil Jackson, former professional basketball player, coach and executive

Coaching Leaders - Share Knowledge, Teach Skills

As the old proverb goes: Give a man a fish and you feed him for a day; teach a man to fish and you feed him for a lifetime. In a broad sense, sharing knowledge and teaching skills is an essential Coaching Leader practice. People learn from you, of course, but they also learn by doing, and in the process develop skills to become more resourceful.

People skills / soft skills

For everyone on your team, even if they are the top experts in their field, emphasize the importance of people skills (soft skills). Mastering people skills is critical for communicating and working with teammates, leaders, colleagues, clients and partners. How we communicate has a huge impact on how we and our message are received. In person, on video calls, in chat and emails, we must all learn how to communicate effectively. Teach, show, do by example.

Start where the person is at

You have likely heard this before. It's a key point about coaching that I learned over time, both in my professional career and as a high-performance driving coach with various car clubs. Start where the person is at, not from where you think they should be or ought to be. Refrain from dwelling on their weak areas or mistakes; evaluate where they are at and address the areas that need improvement. People will appreciate this approach, be more receptive and give you permission to coach. You'll both get better results.

For young professionals and others new to the field, share pertinent information and teach particular skills needed to perform assigned tasks, to focus and meet timelines, and to recognize and flag issues. With more senior resources focus on improvement, innovation, troubleshooting, problem solving, crafting/summarizing reports or presentations, and adding value, including mentoring and coaching. Your top senior resources can make great mentors and coaches as they work alongside others who need a hand. This is extremely powerful in a collaborative environment and creates high-performing teams.

Create collaborative circles

I recommend that you strategize when leading larger teams, say over 100 people, which may include location managers, functional leaders or units of significantly different areas of expertise, skill sets and roles. I would assign pillar leads, e.g., technical leads, functional leads and training coordinators. This creates collaborative circles. Each selected experienced resource would become the go-to person, coach or mentor in a niche. For individuals to be recognized in this way is very gratifying and provides excellent developmental experiences for them. Of course, collaborative circles can serve various purposes, such as cross-pollination and innovation.

Accountability and responsibility

A Coaching Leader must make sure that everyone understands accountability and responsibility. We all have a job to do. When everyone chips in and does their assigned share, things happen and you get results. If someone is struggling, others jump in to help. Phil Jackson also said that the strength of the team is each individual member and the strength of each member is the team.

Resourcefulness and initiative

Coaching people to be resourceful and use initiative is one of the best investments you can make. Motivated high performers don't wait for answers. They dig, reach out to peers, and bring analysis and findings to their leaders for discussion and decisions as needed. This is particularly important with young professionals and emerging leaders. Coach them early on and it will be habit.

I always expected people to do their homework before coming to me. I also always encouraged them to reach out to a teammate because a collaborative team harnesses a vast pool of knowledge and creativity. Encourage R & R (rest and recreation) for well-being and encourage R & I (resourcefulness and initiative) for self-development and growth. Along with a coaching culture, your organization will literally run itself.

Beware of the iceberg of ignorance

I'm not a fan of the adage: "Don't bring me problems; bring me solutions." If people are uncomfortable coming to you because they fear you will judge them as weak or lazy, you may be kept in the dark and the problems may worsen. Even middle managers may not be fully informed by staff.

There's an expression in French: *« Donner l'heure juste. »* Are people giving you the right time of day? Don't be caught; hear them out, engage in the conversation, get the facts. In doing so, you can coach your people by asking questions, sometimes leading them to arrive at options and solutions.

Along the same lines, don't wait for your scheduled call with your boss to raise a critical issue, or to ask for clarification or support on something critical that may hold you and your team back. If there's something your boss needs to know asap, better that it comes from you than an upset customer or another executive.

Be available, be present, be intentional

I've always maintained an open-door policy. Of course, sometimes a leader must focus entirely on a task or activity and needs privacy. We all use "in a meeting" status settings and icons on messaging apps. In a physical office, I sometimes placed a yellow sticker on my door with a simple question, "Can it wait?" Everyone understood and respected the intent: if urgent, knock, and we'll deal with it. This also sets an example for everyone about the need to focus, work on priorities and exercise good judgment.

Coaching Culture – create a ripple effect

Create a coaching culture that reflects the desired mindset and behaviours of Caring Leadership and People First principles while providing your people the opportunity to learn and develop. Coach individuals on your team with the intent of replicating Caring Leadership skills and capability, and of growing more leaders. Coach or provide coaching to all managers and leaders in your organization, including top executives, and yourself. Culture change is a significant undertaking, yet every small positive change counts. *Over time, a Caring Leadership coaching culture will have a ripple effect throughout your organization.* Resulting benefits such as improved listening skills, problem solving, relationships, outcomes and potential growth opportunities can in turn have a positive impact on people's mental health and well-being. Many members of my teams have said that they value the caring coaching relationships from both the work and human perspective.

Managing up and managing down

Managing and strengthening our relationships with our senior leaders is hugely important, at all levels. I think of managing up simply as working more effectively with my boss and managing down as leveraging individual and team strengths. You need to look after both types of relationships and help both parties to be successful. Get to know your boss as an individual, his/her preferences, goals and current concerns. Any information you can provide proactively or a task you can pick up can make a huge difference and will be appreciated. Save some of your valuable 1:1 time to strengthen the relationship, to better understand business drivers, or discuss key topics such as career development. Coach your managers and leaders of leaders to adopt this practice, it helps the entire organisation and makes for a better workplace.

Situational coaching and situational leadership

In the 2019 *Harvard Business Review* article "The Leader as Coach", the authors illustrate different coaching styles. They advise using directive coaching when mentoring, but to aim for a mix of *nondirective coaching and situational coaching. Situational coaching* represents the sweet spot in their framework. All managers in a learning organization should aspire to become experts at situational coaching, which, as its name suggests, involves striking a fine balance between directive and nondirective styles according to the specific needs of the moment.

Ken Blanchard has advocated situational leadership for years, saying, "Leaders, stop treating everybody the same." His company offers *situational leadership* development programs, often marketed as SLII®. An aspect of Blanchard's approach that I find quite clever is its focus on employees and the development they require.

Flip side: Coaching the leader - the power of seeking feedback

> ### LEADER BONUS INSIGHT
>
> Today's leaders need to better understand the power of seeking feedback from their people (allowing them to coach the leader) rather than just thinking it should be a one-way process.
>
> —Patrick J. McKenna, renowned author and strategic advisor

This is a challenge because it's not very commonplace, and it's hard. The fact is, most of us don't like feedback unless it's positive and comforting. Yet constructive feedback can be effective in helping us grow. Of course, *giving feedback* is a leader's responsibility. However, if you are a leader, how often do you *solicit feedback* from your team? The leader must convey that they're open to receiving feedback and asking for suggestions and ways to improve. The tone of voice, body language and words are critical in communication. A trusting relationship must exist before feedback is given honestly, and that depends on the individuals and circumstances. In retrospect, I didn't seek feedback about my own performance as a leader as often as I could have.

"As the person in charge, it's important not only to tolerate receiving negative feedback but to request it and acknowledge its value. Feedback allows you to hear your team's perspective and helps you know how to improve the organization and be a more effective leader."

— Debra Roberts, "To Improve Your Performance as a Leader, Seek Feedback", *Inc.com*

Harvard Business Review has some suggestions on asking for and receiving feedback that can assist you:

- Make it clear you want honest feedback because it will genuinely help you grow.

- Focus on what you can do better in the future rather than on what went wrong.

- Ask questions and be specific about times or areas you require feedback about, such as your effectiveness in yesterday's meeting.

- Listen rather than judge. Becoming defensive makes it less likely that the other person will be honest with you.

There are many facets to being a Coaching Leader as you develop a coaching culture: trust and empowerment, teamwork and collaboration, accountability, responsibility and commitment. Coaching Leaders are also avid readers and learners. Learning is a lifelong journey.

"We—leaders of every stripe—are in the 'Human Growth and Development and Success and Aspiration to Excellence business.' We (Leaders) only grow and succeed when each and every one of our colleagues is growing and succeeding."

— Tom Peters, renowned author of *In Search of Excellence*

EXTRA — A Coaching Leader's guide to effective one-on-one meetings

Here's a practical and structured approach to planning and conducting effective one-on-one meetings, as well as sample questions for both team members and leaders:

1. Schedule one-on-one meetings in advance, possibly with a standing agenda adapted to ongoing work developments or personal needs.

2. Make sure people know what you expect and what they may have to prepare in advance. You may also need to provide something for them.

3. Take good notes. If done remotely, consider using a transcription feature, if available.

4. Respect the time slot set aside for each person: be present, focus on them, show that you *care*.

5. Refrain from offering quick solutions or suggestions. Coaching is primarily done by asking questions.

6. Listen for an answer and wait patiently — sometimes silence is golden. Be sensitive to long pauses that may reflect an inner struggle; give the person time.

7. Ask questions that encourage your team members to reflect and see the answers or options they seek.

8. Cover essential agenda items but leave time at the end for them to use as they wish.

9. For your managers and leaders, make sure to cover their team as well.

10. Consider dedicating some one-on-ones for career development only, say quarterly.

As I've said before, *get to know your people.* Tailor questions and discussions based on the individual and circumstances, and always check-in.

Sample questions for a team member:

1. How are you? How's life? How was your weekend? How is your family?

2. What's working for you this week? Did you inform key people involved of your progress?

3. Do you have a clear understanding of your tasks and end goals?

4. Do you have all the information and support you need?

5. How is your workload? Did you have to work on the weekend?

6. Are some of your commitments in jeopardy, needing more time or someone to step in?

7. What is most crucial/important to you right now?

8. What's NOT working for you this week? Did you inform key people involved of the implications? What steps are you taking to deal with this? Did you ask your colleagues for help? Have you considered approaching this differently?

9. Is there anything that I can help with for you to be successful?

10. What else would you like to discuss – a new client or business opportunity, interests in training, career development, performance, goals, or a personal/family situation that worries you?

Sample questions for a manager/leader, basically the same initial questions PLUS:

1. How is your team? Are you getting to know them personally, something about their family, hobbies?

2. How are morale, teamwork and collaboration in your group? Are people happy to meet with you?

3. Are some of your people struggling with assigned tasks? Are some of your people overextended, jeopardizing their work-life balance? What have you done to help so far?

4. Are some of your projects in trouble? Do you need more resources? Are stakeholders informed?

5. Who are your star performers? Did you praise and share their efforts with other members and leaders as appropriate?

6. Do you have underperformers, and if so, what are you doing to help?

7. Are your senior members mentoring new hires and younger employees?

8. Who should I have a next-level (+1) call with?

9. Do you have anyone at risk of leaving us? Why? Did you discuss this with them?

10. Are you gathering info on key team members you'd like to nominate for quarterly awards, bonus top-ups, promotions or special recognition?

Develop a coaching culture and benefit from the ripple effect. These sessions are often the only way to learn the actual status of things and what may need to be done to make an individual or team successful. For example, I would work with others from my team and my peers to clear someone's calendar so they could succeed with a critical project. There is no point in jeopardizing the outcome of several initiatives because one is sucking up all the cycles. De-escalate, if necessary, then prioritize and reenergize.

BONUS INSIGHTS

Team Member Bonus Insight

How did a leader, coach, or mentor help you to be your best?

First and foremost, the leader acted as a partner in my professional journey. Trust was gained early on and no topic was off limits for discussion. Ideas were bounced back and forth without judgment. Second, my leader was my mentor. Based on a blend of his own experience and my own, the leader put me on a path to advancement and fulfillment. Whether to educate and guide me towards the next step of my career or to assign me to projects that would be challenging and fulfilling, every decision was intended as one step forward. Lastly, and perhaps most importantly, the leader cared about my personal life. Many great leaders will do whatever it takes to see you succeed professionally. But caring to know if my personal life is on the right path makes a world of difference. Work/Life balance is crucial and the life part is easy to forget. Ensuring that I am thriving personally, and work is not a blocker, is paramount to success.

— Steve Aina, Principal Implementation
Consultant, Ceridian

Team Member Bonus Insight

The leader puts me in a challenging role beyond my comfort zone and trusts that I will be able to strive to achieve the goal. I stretch myself to achieve the goals and not let the leader and my teammates down. Looking back, those experiences gave me the best self-improvement and formed the best bond between me and my teammates. The customers benefitted the most by getting the value that's above expectation.

— Evan Zhang, Customer Engineer and Leader,
Google Cloud

CHAPTER 4

Nurturing Human Potential and Building Effective Teams

"The deepest principle in human nature is the craving to be appreciated."

— William James, American philosopher, psychologist and educator

Do you know what motivates every person you interact with regularly? It is practically impossible, but we should try. I've been very fortunate to work with diverse groups of people with varied skill sets across large geographical areas, at times multigenerational and multicultural. We must realize that people's values and motivation may go back to their roots, culture, upbringing and where they are on their life journey. The best way to understand motivation is to get to know people individually and to develop relationships with them. Then you can support, trust and empower them to be successful.

Leading with Care, Empathy and Compassion

While the pandemic may have been a catalyst and accelerator, the Great Resignation, the Great Reflection and the Great Reshuffle started well before that. Various studies and feedback tell us that:

- Retaining and attracting top talent requires understanding what people value. People seek meaningful work in an organization where they are respected, supported and valued.

- More and more people want to engage in something they believe in, a purpose. They want a sense of belonging and to work in an organization whose goals are aligned with their values. This is particularly clear with millennials and Gen Z. Kudos to them! More in Chapter 5.

- Middle managers (manager to vice president) in large enterprises, in particular, are underappreciated, overburdened and stressed, yet they have the most impact on employee engagement and performance. Ironically, most of the leadership development spend is for senior executives.

- We know that people leave bad managers. I did, sometimes leaving an excellent job behind. You may have done, too. People also leave bad jobs and job demands that destroy their work-life balance and threaten their well-being.

"Emotional energy is the true motivation of the human spirit; it's the force of life. When you lead from the heart, your people will follow."

— Mark Crowley, author and leadership consultant

The Head, the Heart and the Hands

You're likely familiar with these metaphors relating to rational and emotional modes of thinking in leadership and people management. It is interesting to look at this with respect to our current volatile conditions in the workplace and our communities. True, we humans are often unpredictable and emotional creatures. By being more caring and empathetic, leaders can better hear what the other person is saying, grasp the underlying meaning, and develop a better working relationship.

A 2013 article in *EHS Today* states: "Whether your natural leadership style is akin to a coach (leading with your heart), a visionary (leading with your head) or an executor (leading with your hands), your approach likely has various benefits and pitfalls." That's undoubtedly true; there is no cookie-cutter leadership type. It is a delicate balance. Most leaders use a combination of the three while being more dominant in one. All can be successful, and of course, it depends. We need visionary leaders (the head) to set the course. This must be done in such a way that everyone understands the vision and their expected contributions. As a Coaching Leader (the heart), I put people first, nurture, equip, trust and empower them. However, we can never lose sight of the team and corporate goals, and the performance required to get expected results. The execution/delivery leader (the hands) gets things done. It requires discipline and focus with realistic targets and without crushing people in the process.

This aligns with my earlier reference to Daniel Goleman's Six Leadership Styles and his conclusion that the best leaders use a combination. Most leadership and coaching roles require *situa-*

tional leadership skills to adapt to various situations, tasks, people and circumstances to meet the needs of both the organization and team members. In all cases, people are the most critical factor!

"Gifted leadership occurs when heart and head—feeling and thought—meet. These are the two winds that allow a leader to soar."

— Daniel Goleman, author and Emotional Intelligence guru

How does Caring Leadership Nurture Human Potential and Build Effective Teams in Practice?

We know that leadership and culture have the most significant impact on employee retention, acquisition, engagement, performance and strategy execution. The best leaders are constantly engaging and coaching people, building relationships and driving to achieve the best results. They develop a culture focused on excellence and client satisfaction. How do they do this? They lead by understanding and leveraging the interdependence of their relationships with their team.

"You can have everything in life you want, if you will just help other people get what they want."

— Zig Ziglar, motivational speaker and best-selling author

What Leaders Want	What Team Members Want
Team members who are cooperative, motivated, trustworthy, competent, skilled, dedicated, highly engaged, high performing, striving to achieve excellence and the best results possible. A leader's responsibilities include both getting results and developing people.	A leader who cares about them, one they can trust and enthusiastically follow, is approachable, trusting, helpful, supportive, and appreciative. A leader willing to train, coach, trust and empower them to succeed, learn and advance their career. An employee's (and team's) responsibilities include delivering results for the organization rather than just showing up.

These simple wish lists are for illustration purposes only and are far from being comprehensive. They may seem at odds and headed for conflict. Not so! They are, in fact, complementary and work wonders when the leader and the team are aligned. In the end, the leader makes it happen. The key is to achieve the goals of the individual, of the team, and of the leader, as well as the overall goals of the organization. Caring Leadership can be a superpower that motivates and empowers people!

Frame corporate goals and employee roles carefully to create high-performing teams

When employees know their contribution helps the company and that the company values them, it's a win-win. Connect people with the vision and purpose; people are proud when they know their work has an impact.

Take an automobile assembly line worker, for example. An individual doesn't just install wheels; that person is part of something bigger. No matter the role or title, people on the assembly line don't just build vehicles, they assemble vehicles with specific features and options to meet a specific order placed by a particular dealership for a very important client — maybe you. A modern vehicle's build sheet includes a long list of items a buyer selected.

The Driving Force: Extraordinary Results with Ordinary People

Peter W. Schutz, former CEO of Porsche AG, is considered "The Man Who Saved the Porsche 911". In his excellent book, Schutz talks about leadership, values, culture, establishing trust and credibility. He gives real life examples of how treating people humanely can inspire and motivate each person to deliver to the best of their abilities. He was a master at getting people's input on achieving goals and getting full buy-in to make it happen. It is the people who make a company successful. Schutz saved Porsche, and he did so with ordinary people, which most of us are. What does that tell you?

EXERCISE: Do a quick assessment of the alignment between what you the leader want and what the team wants. On a scale of 1-10, if it's less than 8, you have work to do. If it is 8 or higher, how can you move it even higher?

Make Architect of People First™ Strategies Work for You

You're likely familiar with the HR-related terms and competencies around leading teams: talent management, retention, acquisition, onboarding, integration, well-being and mental health, employee development, and employee engagement. There's plenty of helpful information out there. Instead, let's look at the following examples applying my **Empowering People through Caring Leadership** principles and see how they can be emulated or adapted to your leadership journey. This approach is similar to my **Empowering Leaders *IN ACTION*** roundtable program focused on what is practical and actionable.

1. Caring Leadership In Action - Develop trusting relationships

Being an effective leader is all about relationships. This includes monitoring well-being. Make it a best practice to check in before starting a one-on-one with staff or colleagues. Many people are hurting and only sincere interest in the other person will bring it out. Check-ins or warm-ups at the start of regular meetings are also a good idea. I always use icebreakers as an introduction for meetings where participants don't know each other. Those few minutes can be fun and boost interaction! Here's one of my favourite icebreakers: if you had an undo or redo button, what is the first thing you would use it for?

When I worked for a leading software company, I was invited by corporate HR as a subject matter expert on "Establishing Trust" as part of their leadership webinar series. I was humbled to have been selected. While in-person interaction is always preferred, these essential practices are equally effective remotely:

- Be kind, personable and open. Lead with care, empathy and compassion.

- Tone of voice, body language and words are all critical. As a leader, people pay attention to what you do, your attitude about things, how you treat others, how often you help out or not, as well as what you say and how you say it.

- Be there to serve and support when needed.

- Sometimes, you can earn trust through sharing, telling stories and being vulnerable talking about life experiences. In doing so, your honesty, integrity and fairness are judged.

- Trust is not the same as respect. People may respect the skills and insights of a leader but distrust their motives.

Trust must be earned. At times, it can be difficult to earn, yet lost so easily. When team members feel safe with their leader and each other, they are comfortable opening up – everyone wins and the team gets stronger.

A related article, "Connect, Then Lead", based on extensive research by *Harvard Business Review*, talks about establishing trust through warmth and understanding. Shari Levitin, author of *Heart and Sell*, says, "Trust is built of five components, but it's empathy that gets you in the door. It's reliability, competency, integrity, and vulnerability that keep you there. But you have to lead with empathy... Before people decide what they think of your message, they decide what they think of you."

2. Caring Leadership In Action – Earn loyalty and attract top candidates

No matter how much authority you have, there are things you cannot command, they must be earned. Trust, respect and loyalty are just a few.

- Money is a top motivator, no question. Caring Leadership increases engagement, performance and loyalty, and helps attract top candidates.

- Retain your people through Caring Leadership with a People First culture where people learn and grow by doing meaningful work aligned with a purpose.

- Attract top talent through your brand and leadership, your story, your purpose and your team. Remember this: candidates are assessing you long before you realize it.

Connect the dots - Caring Leadership holds incredible power *with* people, not *over* people. Empowerment provides opportunities for your people and your organization to grow. Trust and empowerment lead to loyalty and success. *Keep in mind that loyalty is reciprocal.* Many leaders and employees don't get that. One of the most often noted observations made by others as I successfully led high-performing teams was that we had very low attrition. People were motivated, engaged and successful. People stayed.

3. Caring Leadership In Action – Focus on teamwork and recognition

I shared earlier that I created collaborative circles. For the experienced team members who become the go-to person in a "niche", the recognition can be very gratifying. When leading primarily technical or specialized teams, e.g., software engineers, HRMS specialists, being recognized as an expert or thought leader is enormous. In my experience, occasionally someone would volunteer to master a new product or service offering. Once client demand picked up, that skill became sought after by other team members. The early adopters supported and mentored their teammates. Suddenly, these select team members became the go-to people for peer groups, too.

I knew that assuming the abovementioned responsibilities meant extra work for those individuals, some of it on their own time since they were already busy on projects. I acknowledged their contribution and thanked them both privately and openly in the group. It's also good to remind these individuals that the opportunity to lead a collaborative circle is an opportunity to grow and to strut your stuff — make the best of it. Career development is a shared responsibility.

4. Caring Leadership In Action – Drive thought leadership, innovation and strategic enablement through collaboration

We often associate thought leadership and innovation with visionary leaders like Albert Einstein, Steve Jobs and Elon Musk. While few of us are an Einstein, we all have the potential to do great things. Leaders should encourage and cultivate a culture of teamwork and collaboration to drive innovation, thought leadership and strategic enablement. With input from their team, peers, sales, marketing, executive management and customers, the ideas and suggestions brought forward help formulate much better strategies for growth. Such collaboration leads to creative thinking and cooperation in execution.

Each year, my teams would develop comprehensive, future-focused strategic enablement plans, which often kept us ahead of the curve in emerging technologies and upcoming client needs. This strategy enabled our group to maintain a high level of expertise, with some individuals being recognized among the top talent in North America.

5. Caring Leadership In Action - Elevate and motivate

Elevating the level of individual team members elevates the entire team, and advancing the team makes everyone proud to be part of it. Teamwork and accountability are crucial to everyone's success. Celebrate individual and team wins and achievements, big and small.

Monitor key indicators and trends such as revenue generated, utilization, implementations, new leads, and NPS (Net Promoter Score) and share them regularly with the group. At select times, share with other groups and leaders to give your team and its accomplishments more visibility.

For a while, I led a management consulting group involved in smaller strategic assignments that could lead to larger ones for our peer groups. One day, I pointed out that we hit $1 million in revenue. My communication read "The Magic of Small Numbers", addressed not only to my team but to leaders of other teams. Give your people full credit. They deserve it, and they will appreciate it.

While recognized experts and other key members may receive accolades, everyone must first realize they are part of a team. As basketball coach Tom Crean says, "The ambition of being a star can never be greater than your aspiration of playing on a great team."

6. Caring Leadership In Action – Seek and you will find

Seek untapped potential, hidden talent, quiet performers and underappreciated staff. Many leaders only focus their attention on their high performers at the risk of neglecting the rest of their team. The reality is that it takes extra effort and intention for leaders to recognize and develop the quiet ones. Of course, we should support high performers and high potential (HiPo) staff. However, doing so exclusively results in untapped potential in many others who are left behind, feeling like second-class citizens.

Give introverts opportunities and visibility; give both introverts and extroverts airtime. You may be pleasantly surprised. Suddenly, a quiet worker may be recognized as a high performer, an expert or a hero on a client project, perhaps even displaying leadership traits and other potential you weren't aware of. In the process, that person becomes a happier, more engaged and productive employee. Again, a win-win. By the way, check out Susan Cain's excellent book *Quiet: The Power of Introverts in a World That Can't Stop Talking.*

After an organizational change, the previous leaders should provide feedback on staff. In one case, I was advised to assign a woman coming off maternity leave only to projects where she could work from home. However, in our discussion, she indicated she was ready to travel and assume more senior roles where clients needed onsite presence. In cooperation with program directors we made that happen and the feedback was terrific. That person was a star, someone who needed an opportunity to shine. A high performer with previously untapped potential became one of our top team members.

I'll take this opportunity to point out that I've encountered more women being underrated and held back than I have seen men. In fact, I've experienced several men who were overrated, in roles they were not competent for and performing poorly. Leaders, we can do better.

One of the greatest tragedies in life is to watch potential die untapped."

— Myles Munroe, pastor and motivational speaker

7. Caring Leadership In Action – Coach and groom coaches to spur growth

As a Coaching Leader, you help your team members develop and grow in skillset, competence and significance in your organization. You also develop coaches who can, in turn, coach others. Remember to have your coaches check on the other person's well-being, too. Coaching can be on technical skills, people skills, facilitation, client management and sales skills. Even if you're not in a sales organization, you and your teams may need to support business efforts. In many organizations, providing pre-sales and post-sales support is an essential aspect of collaboration. The president of a company I worked for used to say, "Nothing happens until someone sells something."

8. Caring Leadership In Action – Mind your tone, don't bark!

Barking commands at people creates negative stress and anxiety, blurs creative thinking, traps positive energy, demotivates and can lead to depression. Through teamwork and collaboration, leaders can drive innovation and achieve higher performance and results with a happier, more engaged team.

> "Barking orders closes borders. Teamwork and collaboration drive innovation. Self-centred leaders bark orders to scare. True leaders know that the secret is to care."
>
> — Germain St-Denis

9. Caring Leadership In Action – Add some fun!

Laughter is still the best medicine. It's easy to find team building and morale boosting opportunities. Start by asking team members for suggestions. They likely have great ideas.

- Share a daily quote: funny, inspirational, motivational. Take turns.
- Hold an event or an online game challenge.
- Adopt a relevant team name, logo or tag line – for example, a chess piece or a banknote.
- Run a team meeting as a TV show episode or movie scene. We once ran our regional meeting with about 300 people on the bridge of the Starship Enterprise. It was a great team effort. We had tons of fun preparing for and during the event. I got to be Captain Picard leading the meeting, alongside my fantastic crew. As long-time Trekkies, it was an out-of-this-world experience!

10. Caring Leadership In Action – Lead by example

In his book *Three Rules for Living a Good Life,* legendary college football coach Lou Holtz says, "Do the right thing, do the best you can, and always show people you care." I love this simple, practical, and down-to-earth wisdom for everyone and anyone. Lead by example, demonstrating the desired traits and behaviours you expect from your team, and don't ask people to do what you would not do yourself. Be the leader who cares. Be the leader people love to work with.

What do you do to Nurture Human Potential and Build Effective Teams?

There are several other things a leader can do to energize and develop people. What would work for you?

"The biggest leadership lesson I've learned throughout my journey is a word you'll rarely come across in business texts: love. Great leaders love their company, they love their people, they love the mission that they're on. And if everyone in your teams knows that they are going to show up differently tomorrow."

— Pat Gelsinger, CEO, Intel, 2023 Global Leadership Summit

BONUS INSIGHTS

Leader Bonus Insight

My advice – be a storyteller. You can relate to people, coach them, and provide them insights, but the way that people remember is through stories. I host a call every week with about 90 managers. It's grown from 20 people at the beginning to a huge crowd. Every time I think that I will sunset this call, the managers beg me to keep it – I ask what they like about it. They like the updates they get, the management concepts and philosophies I share, they like the interactions with their peers and the guest speakers, but they also like my stories. The stories (mostly) tie in to the topic for the week. Some of my stories are personal, pulled from my family archive – something a kid did that helps demonstrate a behavior I need to talk about (perseverance, transparency), some are from work – dealing with an employment situation in the past that helps demonstrate a management technique, and others are things from history or the news. All are to keep people engaged, to drive a point home, to help them remember. When people feel something in addition to hearing something they are more likely to remember something (repetition helps too). So if I had to give one piece of advice to another leader, I would say to add color to their conversations, tell a story.

— Beth Carroll, Senior Vice President, Global Practices, Ceridian

Leader Bonus Insight

My manager always watched how I was interacting with people and was quick to suggest a different approach. It was how he did that that was pretty amazing. He floated the idea up and had this laugh like he knew you were going to be a little defensive but the laughter took the edge off. And his advice was always insightful. He was always genuine and caring. Being the rebel in the office full of salespeople, he one day said to me, "It wouldn't hurt your career if you sucked up every once in a while." We both laughed because the point was to be nicer to him because without him, I could not have all the latitude he had given me.

Have a fun, caring demeanor with your team. Be the type of leader that doesn't have to wear his or her epaulets on the uniform. Everyone knows you're the boss. They don't need reminding. If they need reminding by you, you may not be the leader.

— Joe Murphy, Vice President Employer
Services, Maximus

Team Member Bonus Insight

That individual would treat me not only as a team member in the workplace but also like one of the extended family members. The individual would give me the opportunity to grow and let me feel that I'm appreciated/valued. The individual with whom I could openly discuss many things including family concerns.

— Kexiong (Sha) Xie, Senior Solution Architect,
TK Elevator Canada

CHAPTER 5

Leading Multigenerational and Multicultural Teams

"How old would you be if you didn't know how old you are?"

— Satchel Paige, American professional baseball pitcher

Does Age Matter?

To be clear: Caring Leadership principles and Architect of People First™ strategies are independent of and transcend age, sex, race, orientation, religion and location. These proven principles concern people, teamwork, collaboration and human connection, *not* stereotyping or artificial divides.

We all learn by dealing with people from across the table, across town, across the country or in another part of the world. I've always lived in diverse communities in the diverse country that Canada is. I had the privilege of working in international development for a while, as well as working with people from various parts of the world, which is common in technology careers. My journey includes mentoring select Master of Engineering university students taking management consulting courses and working with bright new grads, Gen Z and Millennials in a modern and growing tech company. I have led mixed teams of functional and technical professionals and managers with ages varying from 20 to 60. I treated them all the same way, as a Caring Leader. Most people are great, but some are complex, regardless of age.

As a younger professional, I was interviewed for an internal move as a strategic project lead. The discussion was going well, then suddenly the hiring manager stopped and asked, "How do you feel about having older people than you on your team?" I didn't expect that one. My answer: "I don't see a problem." Was the question about me, the older team members, or the hiring manager himself? Was it even necessary? I never entirely understood the question's intent, but it may have been an early foreshadowing of ageism in the workplace.

When is someone too old or too young? It depends, of course, on your perspective. How old must we be to drive a car? When are we too old to drive a car? Hmm… how about looking at one's ability, training, experience, laws, location, roads, culture, economy, social status, etc. This may sound like a kindergarten exercise, but when you think about it, those questions and thoughts, consciously or unconsciously, determine or influence our perspectives, biases and decisions. However, these may also lead us to better decisions and stronger teams.

A March 2023 *Forbes* article "Can 5 Generations Coexist in The Workplace" said, "For the first time in recorded history, there might be five separate and distinct generations in today's workplace… We are in a work world in which a 60-year-old intern is being mentored by a 27-year-old, dispelling the antiquated mindset that only senior employees can be managers."

Recently, I read that automaker BMW (my personal favourite) now has five generations of people working under one roof in their factories, collaborating and contributing their unique skills and perspectives. Of course, we have seen this coming and have had time to prepare for it. Governments, educational institutions and most organizations monitor population and workforce trends.

Meet the Perennials

Instead of slotting people under generational divides, which does nothing but attract attention to gaps and differences, there is a much more innovative way to look at it. If you look up perennials in the dictionary you'll find definitions like "lasting or existing for a long time", "enduring" or "continually recurring". In 2016, Gina Pell, Content Chief of THE WHAT, coined the term *The Perennials*, saying, "We are ever-blooming, curious people of ALL ages who know what's happening in the world, stay current with technology and have friends of all ages." I believe I fall squarely in that category!

In his latest book, *The Perennials, The Megatrends Creating A Postgenerational Society*, Mauro Guillén, Wharton Business School, writes, "A new workforce – individuals who are not pitted against each other either by their age or experience – makes it possible to liberate scores of people from the constraints of the sequential model of life and level the playing field so that everyone has a chance at living a rewarding life."

The authors of *The 100-Year Life: Living and Working in an Age of Longevity* tell us, "Life expectancy is rising, final-salary pensions are vanishing and increasing numbers of people are juggling multiple careers." Kristen Sieffert, President of Finance of America Companies, says, "Future workers could realistically have five (or more) careers in their lifetimes — and never step foot inside an office building, for that matter. This new 'map of life' is certainly a thrilling prospect, but it will also require us to fully embrace the art of reinvention and commit to lifelong learning." (*Fast Company*, November 2022)

These emerging workforce trends should be on your radar. I'll cover them again in Chapter 6 in relation to the Future of Work.

How does Caring Leadership Approach Multigenerational and Multicultural Teams?

How? Not by pointing out differences but by focusing on similarities, on individual and team strengths. Each and every person is a human being who wants to be acknowledged and appreciated.

Leading organizations with multiple generations can be challenging and this remains a hot topic, particularly around Gen Z and Millennials at one end, with boomers and the Grey Tsunami at the other. I've led mixed teams. I do understand that there are differences among generations and that different approaches may be required. However, almost all complexities I have encountered leading people involved the individual, the role, or the organization. Their age or my age was never a factor. The key drivers are leadership style, mindset and communications. Leaders may have to communicate with each age group differently in both providing direction and receiving information or questions. Regardless, leaders and employees must be intentional in understanding and appreciating the multiple benefits of widely mixed organizations.

Whenever I deal with university students, new grads, Gen Z and Millennials, I am always amazed by their energy, enthusiasm, creativity, curiosity and desire to learn. These young professionals and emerging leaders are the future. Take the time to understand what young workers value. You may be surprised to find that their values and ideals are closer to other generations than you realize. Gen Z and Millennials tend to focus on *values* and look for meaningful work at an organization with a purpose they can get behind. They are also intentional about work-life balance, well-being and social responsibility – an admirable mindset! Younger workers simply want to be heard and understood, want to contribute, grow and be successful.

Drop the stereotyping and artificial generational divides

- "How can I possibly lead younger workers or report to them when their values and ideals differ greatly from mine?" They may not be as different as you think. More importantly, maybe you have the ability and experience to be exactly what they want and need you to be. Be a coach or mentor while learning new techniques and tools from younger workers. Work as a team; try reverse mentoring.

- Gen Z and Millennials are not job hoppers. They are motivated and ambitious. It's our responsibility as leaders, experienced professionals, mentors and coaches to understand their goals and support them in their development in the workforce.

- Younger workers don't hurt loyalty — poor leadership and toxic workplace cultures do.

Bring generations together, share your story, and invite them to share

Young workers want to be coached by leaders and experienced workers. Experienced workers are very willing to share their knowledge and acquired wisdom. Be a catalyst and help them both. Show them that you care. Further, younger workers can help older generations keep up with the latest developments and tools, thereby enabling continued or renewed careers. Those with years of accumulated experience and wisdom can help young professionals and emerging leaders get their voices heard and create a better workplace for everyone. Everyone learns while keeping a healthy and diversified perspective.

Leadership Expectations of Young Professionals and Emerging Leaders

In the early stages of the pandemic, some reports suggested that the emergence of younger generations in the workforce, including Millennials and Gen-Z, may have been a key factor in initiating the massive workforce transformation that continues to impact return-to-office policies.

I was invited to participate in a *Leadership and the Future of Work* webinar to talk about "Retaining and Attracting Talent". Participants discussed how to retain and attract top talent during the great resignation. My view was simple: understand what people want and what they value. People want meaningful work in an organization where they are respected, supported, appreciated and aligned with the larger purpose. The underlying premises are that people are happy to work with you and that they enjoy the journey. It's all about creating a culture where employees thrive, leaders thrive and organizations thrive.

Mini survey: Leadership expectations of young professionals and emerging leaders

Sometimes, what we need to know is right in front of us, hiding in plain sight. In 2022, I conducted a mini survey and collected clear insights on what younger generations value and expect from leaders. Respondents were a small representative sample of Gen Z and Millennials I had worked with or mentored. Key points and expectations came across loud and clear:

1. Young professionals want leaders who care and who are willing to invest in them and help them to grow.

2. Most do aspire to be leaders, and almost all would adopt a Coaching Leadership style.

3. All young professionals and emerging leaders believe that anyone can be a leader, with or without a title.

4. Only some are provided with coaching and mentoring in their current roles, most of that to help navigate project issues. None had any learning and development to transition

into leadership roles. This is a severe gap that can influence a person's decision to leave an organization. Leadership development can include management courses or an HR program. However, developmental experiences and coaching (internal and external) have the most significant impact on shaping any potential leader. These may be opportunities to lead a project, rescue an engagement at risk, fill in for a higher-level resource or a manager, or receive accelerated coaching.

5. Leadership style, culture and growth opportunities are the key factors in their decision to join or stay in an organization. Here's what some survey respondents said:

    a) "Leadership style sets the tone for the team."

    b) "I learn from my leaders, and my leader helps me achieve my potential."

    c) "No one likes a crappy boss. I will not stay."

    d) "Bad leadership can demotivate and affect performance."

    e) "Overall, leadership style will make or break the employee."

There you have it, it's very clear. Leaders, the ball is in your court.

- Is this what you see in your organization?
- What are you doing to help your people develop?
- Do you help people develop skills to seize opportunities and demonstrate leadership?
- Are you overlooking untapped potential?

But wait, there was a more extensive survey

As this infographic shows, this much larger survey of 13,382 employees done around the same time in 2022 revealed the top three reasons people leave jobs, and they are all about leadership:

1. Lack of career development/advancement
2. Inadequate compensation
3. Uncaring or uninspiring leader

As this infographic shows, the survey also revealed the most common reasons cited by those handing in their notice. At the top of the list are the classics: "Lack of career development/advancement" and "inadequate compensation." The importance of a good boss is also highlighted, however, with the third most common response being uncaring or uninspiring leaders. A quarter of respondents said that a lack of workplace flexibility was also a factor — an issue acknowledged with varying degrees of enthusiasm and success since swaths of the global workforce realized that working from home was also possible during lockdown.

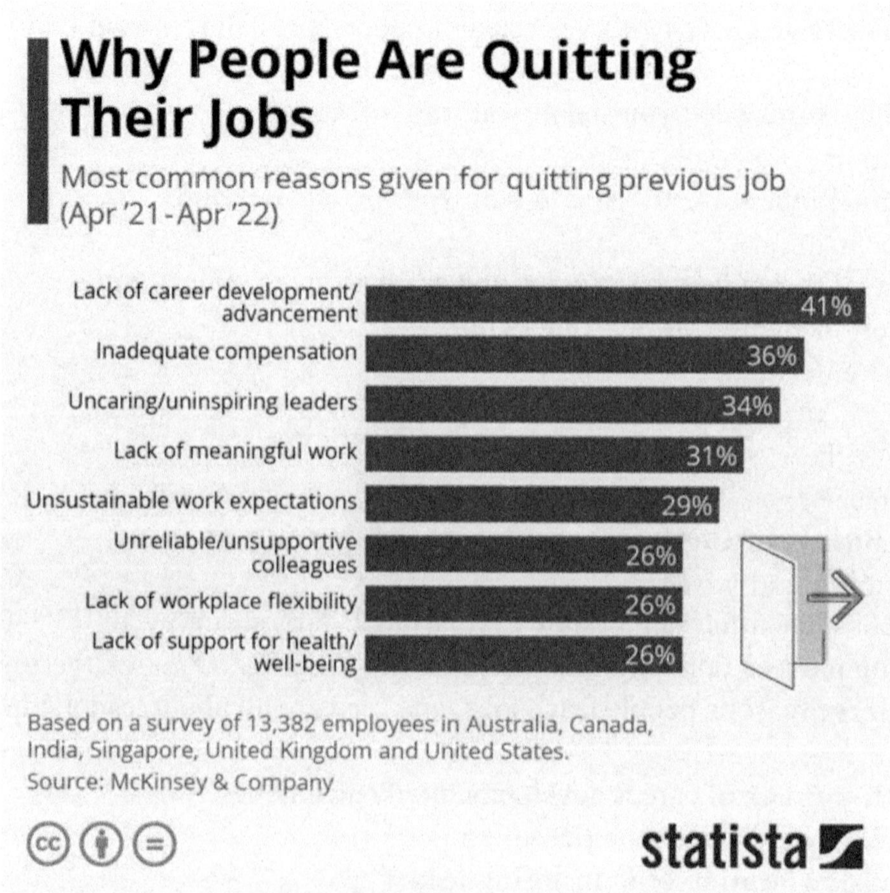

Of course, the two surveys are not comparable. However, it is interesting how the candid responses and insights I received from a small number of people so closely align with the much larger group. The message is clear: *get to know your people!*

> *"Each generation imagines itself to be more intelligent than the one that went before it, and wiser than the one that comes after it".*
>
> — George Orwell, English novelist, author, *Animal Farm*

The Grey Tsunami

The so-called grey tsunami refers to the large wave of baby boomers who are reaching retirement age. How should we view this in the workplace? Is our aging population who are departing contributing to our talent shortage, or could they be part of the solution? While many older workers decided to retire or leave a job in the early stages of the pandemic, many of them are now re-entering the workforce.

As the recent business commentary about perennials suggests, age is no longer relevant to organizational success. It's more about capability, adaptability, skills, motivation, acquired experience and wisdom that can be shared. Cost of living, inflation, household debt and a desire to contribute and to be with others are some of the reasons why so many workers can be considered perennials in the workplace. Some workers need the money to make ends meet and to enjoy a quality life. Others may be looking for a new job and are pursuing second careers. These individuals look for full-time employment that will generate a steady income. Still others may prefer interim, part-time roles or occasional engagements. In an established firm or a start-up, the following temporary roles can be a win-win:

- A facilitator or speaker for upcoming meetings
- A good listener who can act as a sounding board
- A mentor or coach
- A change or transformation strategist
- Someone who's been there, done that, and is good at problem-solving

These ever-blooming perennials who remain curious and eager to learn new work methods and the latest technology can join a team that needs more people to achieve its goals.

Passing the Baton

Finally, when discussing aging populations, don't forget succession development and succession planning. Someone with experience can help develop the next top performer or the next leader. When workers leave it creates a void for another skilled worker to fill. Before leaders go or plan to leave, they should have developed a successor or a selection of potential candidates for their replacement.

I close with this fabulous quote my friend Doug Dawson wrote as a comment on one of my blog posts: "We were not designed with a finish line in mind; rather, a purpose to accomplish."

TEAM MEMBER BONUS INSIGHTS – GEN Z AND MILLENNIALS

How did a leader, coach or mentor help you to be your best?

Under my manager's guidance, I was able to take part in high-visibility projects and had the opportunity to receive coaching and provide mentorship to other junior consultants.

— Tina Zhang, former consultant, MBA candidate, University of Michigan Ross School of Business

> The individual built up my confidence and exposed me to real-life experiences rather than keep me in the shadows.
>
> — Erica Parisi, Senior Consultant, Digital Workforce Transformation, EY
>
> The most important aspect I would say is that they had my back at work and set me up to do well, as opposed to setting unrealistic expectations.
>
> — Tas Hoque, Consultant, Technology - People Experience, BDO Canada
>
> He trusted me with the work and did not micromanage.
>
> — Imtiaz Khan, Senior Consultant, Dayforce WFM, BDO Canada

CHAPTER 6

The Future of Work: The Human Connection and Work Relationships

"First and foremost, I believe in flexible working. It is important that employers appreciate their employees' work-life balance and give them the flexibility to work around their personal lives."

— Sir Richard Branson, Founder, Virgin Group

Why include a chapter on Hybrid Remote and the Future of Work in this book? Isn't the pandemic over and things are back to normal? Things may not settle for quite a while and the implications on people and organizations are still being ironed out. What is normal anyway? What will be the next normal with the rapid pace of change, innovation and advancement of technology, including Generative AI? In some ways, we are all *co-creators* of the Future of Work. Every organization, leadership team and individual has an opportunity to help create a better workplace for everyone.

From a workforce perspective, the pandemic was a huge experiment with some good coming out of it as well as some lingering issues. The key considerations remain the human connection and relationships. It's not about where people work but about how people work together in an organized environment to foster collaboration and human interaction to accomplish set goals, regardless of base location. It's about creating conditions where remote, hybrid and onsite workers and leaders can succeed, and where the organizations they work in can succeed. For that to happen from a Caring Leadership and People First point of view, the human connection must always be reinforced, in person and remotely, and work relationships must evolve in this new paradigm.

Perspective on Hybrid / Remote Work - Virtual Versus Visible

Do you and your boss work in the same physical location, same city, same country? The last time my boss and I were in the same office was mid-2008, with only some of our staff in the same town. In fact, the last time I was co-located with my boss and all members of my staff was in the 1990s. Of course, it's great to work alongside colleagues and managers. However, unless you work in a small organization or one that is regionalized, where everyone comes to the same office, your team may be located in other cities and other countries. Is this a concern for you?

In 2020, I had the privilege of working at a growing tech company. With pandemic restrictions newly in place, everything was done remotely. The more senior staff seemed to cope well enough; however, this situation was very challenging for younger workers and new grads, some of whom were starting their very first job, working in whatever accommodation they had for university, sometimes only a bedroom or shared apartment. Virtual meetings via Zoom and Teams became our go-to communication vehicles. They effectively bridged the geographical divide and provided physical distancing, yet those tools are no replacement for direct, face-to-face interactions.

Even though we were blessed with good jobs while other people were being let go, something was missing. At my three-month milestone, I decided to do something different. With restrictions easing and the approval of the crisis management team, I invited local members of the team for lunch on a patio... yes, in person, face to face. Even with masks and precautions, it was a most rewarding experience for everyone. Around that time, I loved the comment made about video calls by a witty older friend who lamented, "You can't hug those little squares!"

A perspective that's often missed is that the imposed restrictions and rushed work from home experience under COVID-19 restrictions was quite different from previous remote work scenarios. Before restrictions, in-person onsite meetings, events, leadership meetings and team get-togethers were part of the mix to strengthen collaboration and the human connection. Everyone understood that remote/hybrid work required flexibility, accountability, respect of boundaries and acceptance of unexpected interruptions. The restrictions imposed during the pandemic skewed people's understanding of remote work. The isolation, lack of trust and inexperience with remote work left many with a distorted picture. We all need in-person interaction.

You may have heard of the concept of hotelling. The company I worked for when I lived in Ottawa implemented it because we ran out of office space during a growth spurt. Leaders (including me) approved select staff members to work from home when they were not at a client location and did not need to be in the office or interact with colleagues in person. For many, working remotely was a good environment to do concentrated work independently, just like it can be today. Now get this: The integrity, commitment to the job and productivity of our employees were never questioned. We trusted employees implicitly and the results never disappointed. This is a testament to strong leadership in a people-oriented culture with high-performing teams.

> *"To start building your remote culture, establish and share some basic rules. The first and most important rule is mutual trust between the company and its workers. The rules after that? As few as possible."*
>
> — Larry English, author, *Office Optional*

From my experience leading diverse virtual teams — hybrid, remote and onsite — across a wide geography since about 2008, leadership still boils down to the same things. Effective remote work requires discipline and organization, strong relationships, trust and collaboration. How we do things and how we communicate, in particular, is different. Although those new to remote work may have experienced the common performance dip due to the change, perseverance and strong communication can lead to a highly productive remote or hybrid team. Of course, it's not for everyone, for every role or every home situation.

Noteworthy observations and considerations from the pandemic:

1. A positive outcome of the pandemic is that understanding, caring, empathy and compassion have taken centre stage. We could argue that things should have been that way all along. A key reason is that leaders went along because they,

too, were in the same boat, and had to cope in the same way their staff did. Will this remain so going forward or will some bullies charge again? There are lingering signs of depression and anxiety from the isolation and challenges of the pandemic. Caring Leadership can prove to be a godsend for those employees going forward. They could fall apart under authoritative commanding leaders who have little concern for people's well-being.

2. Organizations with women leaders appeared better at understanding the impact of the pandemic in terms of the needs of employees and of the organization to help them get through a difficult period. I don't mean just accommodating mothers with young children which, of course, is a must. Generally, women leaders seem better than many men at recognizing signs of employees struggling or approaching high levels of stress. Will more organizations put more caring women in leadership roles? With a few exceptions, I've found women leaders to be highly competent and superb to work with. Erin Thorp, author of *Inside Out Empathy,* says, "Leading with empathy and creating inclusive environments means that, as leaders, we create space for questions to be asked."

3. Some organizations have chosen to make remote work permanent, seeing clear benefits such as no commute and reduced office space costs with sustained performance and results. Most organizations provide suitable space for people to get together to brainstorm, review progress or even just hang out together. Again, for less experienced employees, new graduates and new hires, full-time remote work can be a challenge. These employees often need to work side-

by-side with colleagues and project teams to understand workflows, build relationships and develop confidence.

4. Many organizations are now asking, even mandating, that people return to the office. Return to office policies are being sorted out with some resistance from remote workers. Increased flexibility from both sides would help. I love the term "intentionally flexible" (coined by an IBM executive, I believe), meaning based on the need of the employees and the organization at a given time.

5. For many other organizations, hybrid work models seem to be an appealing compromise, combining remote and in-office days. This will likely become the standard of the future. To make this work effectively, leading organizations will emphasize collaborative circles that reflect the nature of the work and the needs of the workforce. They will offer various types of physical workspaces and encourage or arrange in-person get-togethers to provide ample opportunities to satisfy our fundamental need for human connection. However, there are a few things to watch for in a hybrid arrangement; it has the potential to create a tiered culture that leaves remote employees feeling like they are second-class. Will in-office employees remember to include their remote colleagues in discussions and decisions that impact them? Will bosses tend to favour those around them, a tendency commonly referred to as "proximity bias"?

6. Hybrid remote work and return to office policies solely based on the pandemic experience are missing key parts of the equation and missing out on opportunity. With hybrid work, you can access a broader talent pool. You can easily

invite remote colleagues and customers to join virtual calls and participate in key discussions. You can deliver value to clients remotely in addition to face-to-face meetings.

7. The shift to remote work has led to a significant emphasis on employee engagement, with many companies implementing frequent touch points and one-on-one calls. This approach is and always was a best practice, especially for more junior staff. However, overdoing it can lead to unnecessary meetings and a dependency which reduces resourcefulness. It's important to strike a balance, allowing employees to work independently and to learn by researching and figuring things out on their own.

8. Another crucial aspect to consider is the discipline required to maintain work-life balance and ensure employee well-being. Being engaged in work and ready to respond at all times can blur the lines between work and personal life. It's essential for companies to set boundaries that respect "on" and "off" hours and promote a healthy work/life balance. By the way, leaders are people too and they also need to unplug. How companies tackle this issue will be a defining factor in their success moving forward.

9. Many organizations and leaders are struggling to effectively lead remote teams and don't dare ask for help, afraid they may appear weak or inept. In my coaching and consulting practice, helping leaders learn to develop relationships remotely, to facilitate remote meetings, and to lead change from afar across organizational boundaries are top priorities.

10. Honesty and transparency can go a long way. Leaders who prefer people in the office because it's their leadership style and it's best for the type of work being done should simply say so. Same for organizations with empty office space that they pay for under contractual agreements that cannot be changed quickly. There is no single ideal arrangement, it just depends. Whatever the case, flexibility in the chosen approach may be king.

Bottom line is that geographical distance or proximity should not hinder the potential for effective impactful leadership. Whether people work onsite, remote or in a hybrid work environment, the critical in-person interactions benefit all workers and leaders tremendously. Of course, we must manage discretionary expenses. However, using travel costs as a barrier to leaders visiting their team members and to holding team get-togethers is a pathetic excuse compared to the benefits of trusting relationships, teamwork, employee engagement, performance and loyalty. Such policies and directives reflect *uncaring* leadership and culture.

Out of sight should NOT mean out of mind!

Here is another key point I believe merits emphasizing: while leaders need to be intentional and flexible in establishing policies, *all workers* at all levels need to understand that they too play a role in making this work effectively. There are employees who abuse the privilege of being "out of sight" while working remotely. Their behaviour and immaturity can negatively impact everyone. In a chapter he wrote for a university textbook published by IGI Global in 2022, Doug Dawson says, "Employees want to feel valued and significant. How leaders approach the challenges of the hybrid workforce determines whether or not an employee feels empowered, included and ultimately, significant." This is a great segue into the second part of this chapter - work relationships.

Advancing the Future of Work - The Human Connection and Work Relationships

Do you need a Chief Remote Officer? How about a Chief Future of Work Officer? Maybe the responsibilities are handled by your Chief People Office, your HR leader or another leader. The title is not as significant as the role and support behind it.

The idea of having someone in a position of authority to focus on what, where, why and how we work could prove most beneficial. It's time to stop focusing so much on where people work and look at the broader picture and work relationships. The pandemic was not the only driver of change in the workplace. Innovation, technology, social and economic pressures all drive change. The main factors are the nature of the job, daily tasks and interactions required. In simplest terms:

"The best way to predict the future is to create it."

— Abraham Lincoln, 16th President of the United States

Tsedal Neeley, Harvard Business School, says, "You now have a workforce predominantly working online: You need new ways of thinking about recruiting, training, developing and promoting employees. It represents a radical shift in the management, design and culture of a company, so having someone in charge of it is smart."

As Head of Remote, Chase Warrington ends up spending much of his workday focusing on the in-person experience. "I'm in charge of our company offsites – it's crucial to have a good IRL [in-real-life] strategy among distributed teams," he explains. "Human connection was the top priority when I took the role." Warrington leads the remote strategy for productivity software firm Doist.

In earlier chapters we mentioned the importance of understanding people's values. People want to engage in something they believe in, a purpose, a belonging, to work in an organization whose goals are aligned with their values. All of this points to the human connection and work relationships.

Over 10 years ago, world-acclaimed leadership expert Dave Ulrich and psychologist Wendy Ulrich wrote *The Why of Work,* a book about creating meaning and value in the workplace. One of their conclusions reflects a perspective on society that I fully endorse: "According to studies, we all work for the same thing, and it's not just money. It's *meaning.* Through our work, we seek a sense of purpose, contribution, connection, value and hope. Digging down to the meaning of work taps our resilience in hard times and our passion in good times."

The Future of Work is Human - Human Capability and Work Relationships

- Developing human capability means investing in people and your organization, and living your values. Various organizations are pointing to the some of their own initiatives and research.

- Dave Ulrich says, "Human capability is the human, that's the talent, capability is the organization, and when you manage those, you serve your employees really well. They're committed, they're competent, they're productive. You serve your line managers, you serve yourself. You build an organization that wins but you also serve your customers. You serve your investors..."

- Margaret Stuart, Country Manager, Salesforce Canada, talks about values-driven leadership and a survey that shed light on the values that Canadians believe are paramount to successful leadership today, regardless of gender.

- From research findings shared by HP CEO Enrique Lores, only about a quarter of employees feel they have a healthy relationship with their work, receive the respect and value they deserve, or have a clear sense of purpose, empowerment and genuine connection to their work. Only *one quarter*.

- In a reversal of policies, CEO Raul Vargas told employees that he'd require the majority of Farmers Group staff to work in the office three days a week to further collaboration, creativity and innovation.

- An October 2022 article in *BBC Worklife* introduces an interesting and promising approach of non-linear workdays and working asynchronously – keeping different hours than their colleagues. Key points are: "Some employees are breaking up their working days into a few hours at a time, doing tasks flexibly and asynchronously in the new world of work... The hope is that if employers can introduce non-linear workday policies more formally, it'll redress the balance between asynchronous work and overwork."

- It's easy to see how all this ties into a key message of the previous chapter: people are living longer, healthier lives, embarking on multiple careers and ever blooming.

These developments could be considered an extension of the hybrid work we've experienced morphing into a more formal arrangement. In reality, the need for change has been there for some time and the way we work is evolving. Obviously, the next normal will require utmost adaptability, flexibility, trust, empowerment and accountability. Add to this the fact that more and more people work as independent contractors in the gig economy. Where will they work from? Does it matter?

We have an opportunity, perhaps a responsibility, to revaluate and redefine work, and better align both the organizations and the people that make them successful. Driving change in our uncertain times means focusing on how we can enable all leaders today to take an authentic, values-driven approach to leadership. How one source defines values-driven leaders seems ideal, but not easy to achieve: "Values-driven leaders lead from a deep sense of purpose and a demonstrated commitment to life-affirming values, such as honesty, integrity, excellence, courage, humility, trust, care for people and social and environmental responsibility."

The future is uncertain, but one thing remains clear: *human connection and personal interaction are irreplaceable.* They forge trust, enable collaboration and facilitate conflict resolution. The future of work may be digital, but it will always need a human touch. We need to find the balance between leveraging the potential of new ways of work regardless of location and nurturing our inherent need for human connection. An open mind and flexibly are certainly required mindsets.

Moving forward requires comprehensive strategies and practical, collaborative approaches that can adapt to the evolving workplace where people and businesses grow and prosper. That is beyond the scope of this book, of course. However, I hope that reading this chapter helped heighten your awareness, and your creative juices are flowing with ideas to explore further.

The link between Caring Leadership, workplace culture and performance is clear. Key attributes of future leaders are the ability to work with different people, flexibility to adapt to different situations, and a sense — a gut feel or intuition — that they and their team can accomplish amazing things.

Key Takeaway - Caring Leadership Strategies for the Future of Work

The Future of Work transcends the physical confines of the office. It's about creating an environment that:

a) Values employees, cares for them and ensures their well-being

b) Develops, equips, trusts and empowers people

c) Provides productive and engaged organizational capability to meet the goals of the organization

Serve your people and they will serve your customers. All leaders and organizations need to understand that caring, empathy, compassion, trust, empowerment, teamwork, collaboration, flexibility and adaptability are the new currencies of the modern workplace.

"The way we work will change significantly in almost all functions and will require new skills. Social, emotional and technological skills will become more important."

— Julia Sperling-Magro, Partner, McKinsey

BONUS INSIGHT

Team Member Bonus Insight

Work-life balance is often discussed, but managers often overlook it when it comes to meeting deadlines. This is especially true for working moms. Managers fail to take concrete measures to ensure a good balance, which can be disheartening. They ignore personal circumstances, set unrealistic expectations, lack flexibility, and don't provide support systems. This discourages the establishment of boundaries between work and personal life. The situation is unfortunate because it puts hardworking and ambitious moms in a difficult position where they have to choose between a healthy family life or a successful career. In many organizations, the definition of success is often associated with the ability to work endless overtime without complaining. This expectation can be detrimental to the well-being and work-life balance of working moms, creating a challenging dilemma that should be addressed and rectified.

— Haneen Samara, manager, Digital Workforce Transformation, EY

PART THREE:

Putting Caring Leadership into Practice

CHAPTER 7

Dealing with Tough Stuff Using a People First Mindset

"Life isn't about waiting for the storm to pass; it's about learning how to dance in the rain."

— Vivian Greene, American author and entrepreneur

A leader wears many hats. Most are light, bright and tasteful, and you like to wear them daily. *Life is good.* The biggest, heaviest, ugliest hats are for the tough stuff. You need them to deal with the most complex challenges and responsibilities of leadership. *Life can be a bitch.* Some hats won't fit you well, but you may have to use them at certain times in your leadership journey. When you do, you must keep your people in mind. Every decision you make or don't make can have a tremendous impact on people's careers and lives. Remember the Golden Rule of Leadership and put People First.

This chapter covers several key takeaways and lessons learned from experience. These are based on true stories that I and others have been through. Being a leader has been very rewarding; however, I faced challenges and tough times I never imagined I would. You may also. How you deal with these impacts you, your people and your organization. Here are three key areas:

- Dealing with people issues of every stripe
- Dealing with crises, M&As, reorganizations, layoffs
- Providing Change Leadership - navigating change, disruption and transformation

Life is Hard – We are Only Human

We all have times when we feel life is hard or see others struggling. In his book *Life is Hard,* MIT Professor Kieran Setiya shares his insights based on advanced studies to help us understand ourselves and our fellow human beings. As a Caring Leader, parent or friend, being genuinely intentional about understanding, acknowledging and accepting certain situations can make a world of difference. Sharing can help, too. Sharing our own life challenges can not only help you, but it can help your people open up and even release some of their burdens. I tend to have a positive outlook, which has always helped me through life's trials and tribulations. I'm also realistic. In a challenging situation, I tell myself it won't last forever, it will pass. Equally, when we are blessed, we must realize that it can be taken away. Life is like that!

When life challenges, work-related or not, come up within your team, the ability to manage the situation is crucial for you as the leader. Calm and reflection are clearly better than knee jerk reactions.

As incredible as it may seem, two members of my teams have had brain surgery on my watch. They were on different teams at different times. Core elements of support to the employees from both the company and the insurance provider were facilitated effectively by HR, thankfully. Yet, I felt a personal need and obligation to support each person. This involved check-ins with them and their spouse to see how they were doing and later to support the transition back to work, as they both recovered fully. It was the least I could do, not only as a manager but as a fellow human being. I cared and they appreciated it.

Family responsibilities are part of life and can impact capacity and performance. When situations requiring urgent attention arise, arrangements must be made quickly with stakeholders (peer organizations, clients, account teams, senior management). In today's virtual meeting madness, we happily make space for these as much as we can. Other challenges are not so straightforward:

- A peer, client or account representative tells you they want a particular staff member removed from a project. Ugh, that's a tough one. What is the issue? Personalities, competence, team dynamics? You want to avoid impacting the business or destroying a team member but must move swiftly to reassure stakeholders. You also need to have a good talk with the person. What is the lesson here? Thankfully, I had few of these. I always tried to be as strategic as possible about assigning resources that best fit the task, the people (internal and external) and the project environment. This approach always paid off.

- A staff member decides that he is no longer willing to work on a project or travel to out-of-town clients. One can't arbitrarily decide this. What is the underlying problem?

- One of your team members is being bullied by a program executive. Not acceptable!

- Then there's the poor performer who enjoys a close relationship with your boss. This is tricky but manageable and must be addressed.

Being a supportive, caring, empathetic and compassionate leader matters. Yet you must be firm and do what's best for all involved. Your people will appreciate your support and will pay you back in spades. Your boss and stakeholders see you take responsibility. That matters, too.

Stuff Happens

"There is no education like adversity."

— Benjamin Disraeli, Former Prime Minister of the United Kingdom

As they say, running a well-oiled machine is relatively easy. The fun starts when the unexpected happens, when something other than fresh air hits the fan! Things begin to break, veer off the road, or run into a wall. In those situations, character comes into play. Adversity can bring out your natural leadership and character strengths.

While the COVID pandemic was unprecedented, some of us have been through other significant crises: the Dot Com bust, the business impact of the September 11 terrorist attacks, the 2008-2009 economic recession, health crises (self and staff), and more… all seriously impacting people at home and in the workplace. Similarly, mergers and acquisitions, major reorganizations and leadership turnover profoundly affect people, potentially changing people's lives. Let's look at the following situations:

Mergers and acquisitions (M&A) - The acquisition of the consulting firm I worked for in Ottawa was my first M&A experience. Key leaders left, including those I dealt with at head office, and the vibe changed. Our region continued to hum along successfully, but the company's direction was unclear. We'd lost our mojo.

A promising new job and a botched acquisition - As the new millennium rolled in, I started a new role as Canadian vice president for a newly formed e-business consulting firm. The parent company had bought some smaller companies in Canada and the U.S. for this new venture. My first task was to evaluate the business and people in each of the three offices in Canada. I found a significant misalignment due to a poor acquisition strategy, leaving me with a big mess to sort out. I had to decide which units to fold in the new venture and which units to drop. Sadly, some people lost their jobs as their units were shut down. Letting people go is never easy as a leader. I was in the Toronto location, which had a good book of business, a solid team of expert consultants and an experienced location manager. That team was previously run by the person who became my boss, our North American leader. As you'd expect, that office was in good shape. We needed more people to make our numbers and started hiring staff, including more senior strategic advisors for our clients and a new location manager for the Montreal office. We were doing well and everything looked very promising. Life was good, until 9/11.

Terror and tragedy - On September 11, 2001 tragedy struck. The terrorist attacks on the World Trade Center's Twin Towers unleashed horrors of the worst kind. The world stopped; thousands died needlessly. The impact of 9/11 was felt everywhere and on many fronts. It had a significant impact on our U.S. and Canadian clients. A good portion of our clients were in the U.S. and our business dropped and dropped. Our parent company lost confidence in the market. We had to let people go, some of whom we had hired within the year. I had to close the Montreal office. It was a tough, sad day as I faced them in a small meeting room. Not much later, it was my turn to go. Boom! They didn't need a vice president for Canada with only one office and dwindling business — another tough blow. My only consolation was that we did all we could and treated everyone with the respect they deserved.

A third M&A experience - In 2008, at a meeting with some of our current executives before the legal entity change, one key message resonated with me: you will need diverse skills to face upcoming challenges. Sage advice. Adversity builds resilience. People build resilience and the ability to manage change, adapt and persevere. We went from a close-knit Canadian unit of approximately 40 people in a company of about 5,000 employees to a fragmented group slotted in a behemoth organization of over 100,000 employees. The experience of our U.S. counterparts was similar. Few of the sales staff transitioned over. Clients were calling me looking for clarity and guidance, but I didn't know much more than they did.

Our first meetings with leaders from the acquiring company were rocky – a real culture shock! As you'd expect, our people raised several questions. One time, a leader became frustrated and said (I paraphrase), "If you don't like it here, you don't have to stay." Yikes! Talk about making the team feel unimportant. More like motivating them to abandon ship. Where's that warm welcome you'd expect as new employees? We had moved from a team-oriented, friendly culture to an authoritative dog-eat-dog culture. Thankfully, we had an excellent transition partner who helped us through the murky waters. As we settled in, we soon realized that the processes in this company were overkill for some of the contracts we had and the opportunities we were pursuing. With my usual good humour, I coined this expression: "You don't need an 18-wheeler to move an envelope."

A few words of advice when entering a new venture:

- Take time to learn the landscape, the players, the ecosystem, patterns and unwritten rules.
- Ask questions and listen to people; listen to your team.
- Learn as much as you can.
- Gain respect, credibility and trust by consistently being authentic and helping your team and the organization succeed.

We went through several reorganizations and executive churn. One time, members of my team and of peer teams were transferred to another part of the company without our knowledge. Our people were not happy and we leaders were not happy. We needed them and we fought for months to eventually bring them back.

"Fight for the things that you care about but do it in a way that will lead others to join you."

— Ruth Bader Ginsburg, Former Associate Justice of the Supreme Court of the United States

Putting People First - Fortunately, my team continued to perform well and gave me their full cooperation, as always, even when we had to do things differently. I removed as many hurdles as I could and appreciated their loyalty. I was asked a few times to take on a different role. I chose to stay with my team and help them out. I was able to work for my team in the background to give them visibility and recommend high performers for awards and promotions. We even had multiple success stories on the corporate website. A senior colleague once told me, "If you continue to focus on your people, you'll never get ahead." Well, so be it.

The organization remained a difficult corporate culture for me with many authoritarian, commanding leaders. One executive had a reputation for being tough; apparently, people feared him. During a recession, slowing demand for our expert consultants was a real concern for all of us. Jobs were at stake. This individual initiated an extended sales program with delivery managers and leaders taking on sales responsibilities. When I found out, I volunteered to join U.S. leaders as the representative for Canada. We also needed more business in Canada to avoid layoffs. It turned out to be a great experience. I knew many of our key clients, but not their possible needs for our services. I asked my people to send me names of clients who possibly needed expert assistance. After several unsuccessful calls, bingo! That approach proved successful and we signed new business. In the process, something tremendously valuable developed. I established credibility and good relationships with other leaders, including the one that people feared. I subsequently received and appreciated his support on several occasions. I truly appreciated how my team supported my efforts and hung on during those difficult times.

The message here is never give up, be humble, reach out for help and make the best of your situation. Lean into frustration and obstacles, jump on opportunities to make a difference, and take ownership. You never know how things will turn out. Despite the challenges, overall, I was fortunate to work with good leaders and have stayed in touch with some of them, as well as former colleagues. *My team and my ability to work with people were always my secret weapons.* Leadership rests on basic principles of human understanding.

"Life consists not in holding good cards
but in playing those you hold well."

— Josh Billings, author and philosophical humorist

Change Leadership - Navigating Change, Disruption and Transformation

Much of what we do in business involves change, and almost everything we do as leaders involves change and the people involved. Change leadership (as opposed to change management methodologies) from top leaders requires communicating clear objectives and purpose (why we're doing this) and what it means to impacted employees and clients. Early involvement by all stakeholders is critical. However, we all tend to naturally resist change. It may come from our personality, upbringing, culture, religion, community, etc. *You can't lead change effectively if you can't lead people effectively.* Create a culture of trust and accountability, where people can ask questions and even challenge without fear of reprisal.

> *"It is not the strongest species that survive, nor the most intelligent, but the most responsive to change."*
>
> — Charles Darwin, naturalist and father of evolutionary theory

Without question, the pandemic was the most powerful driver of change and innovation in 2020. Not CEOs, CIOs, futurists or strategists. Why? Because we had to! This rapid pace of change and technology adoption actually started pre-pandemic; however, the failure rate for major transformation initiatives was high, with some organizations reporting a 70% failure rate. Add COVID-19 to the fire and we were living in a VUCA world — volatile, uncertain, complex and ambiguous. People were left struggling, worried, disengaged and discouraged. Carolyn Swora, leadership expert with two books on VUCA and leadership, says, "We can't show up as our best selves when our nervous system is wrecked." Leaders must be very aware of this and give it due consideration to help people cope and to succeed generally. Leaders must also care for themselves, i.e., put your oxygen mask on first.

If the pace of change and innovation is faster than people can adapt, adoption is slowed and can be potentially jeopardized by workarounds and negative patterns. The most crucial needs of people impacted must be addressed to get the behavioural changes so essential for true adoption. What's in it for me? Will I lose my job? This is too difficult for me! In the end, everything boils down to actual adoption by people. Poor adoption of technology or other change initiatives can negatively impact an organization, its leaders, employees and customers.

An excellent Change Leadership question might be: are you looking at change through the right lens? As organizations undergo change and transformation, not all critical success factors are created equal. You need to look through two critical lenses for successful change: *business capability* and *human capability.* Business imperatives will usually drive change, with leaders setting objectives and plans to operationalize the new mode of operation. At the same time, the people involved and impacted need to understand the vision and implications on them, their roles and duties. Early involvement of those people creates an opportunity to make the solution better for both customers and employees.

Mind the Dip - Of course, be prepared for the inevitable performance dip, aka the dreaded valley of death. Take steps to minimize the performance and productivity dip that comes with major change initiatives. People are very adaptive, but we're also creatures of habit, tending to go back to business-as-usual decisions and assumptions. When all that changes, productivity dips temporarily. Manage it, don't stay there, and move on. Every new undertaking looks like a failure in the middle. Here is a personal quote I coined a few years ago:

> "The degree of success and real benefits derived from any transformation, innovation and disruptive technology is directly related to effort and attention focused on getting people to effectively adopt it."
>
> — Germain St-Denis

One of the best books on leading change is Michael Leckie's *The Heart of Transformation*, an excellent practical guide to transformation with a human-centric approach. Recognized as a "digital transformation leader", Michael is passionate about change and transformation and puts People First.

Quick to Hire, Quick to Fire!

While exercises and techniques such as rank-and-stack and 9-box grid for evaluating people's performance and potential can be quite useful, they may be a disguise for layoffs - RIFs (reduction in force). They can be companywide or specific to particular groups or regions.

The technology sector is still immature, with a quarterly focus on profit over people. It can go from talent shortage and knee-jerk hiring to staff surplus and layoffs almost overnight, not necessarily because of crises. It's a mindset; people are considered a commodity. For example, at the end of 2021, Microsoft CEO Satya Nadella said that *employee care* was the new currency, yet a year and a half later thousands of his employees were being laid off. Everyone understands that market conditions change. For those impacted, you can't say it's not personal, it's business. *It is personal and it hurts.* Leaders and managers, do as you must, but please have a heart and show some compassion and respect.

While it is common practice to track employee engagement and satisfaction through surveys, it may be executive churn that kills employee motivation and loyalty. In my corporate jobs, sometimes a new executive (senior or executive vice president) would come in every 18 months. Enough time to develop a strategy perhaps, but never enough to see it through. Employees become disinterested. I did my best to keep my teams focused on their work. People value management continuity.

The best strategy is to keep yourself fresh: reskill and relearn. Learning is a lifelong journey. Always keep up with new developments, new ways of learning, and strongly encourage your people to do so as well. New relevant knowledge and skills may help you deal with or even avoid some nasty situations. Today, it's all about artificial intelligence (AI). AI may take over fewer jobs than people fear but the people using AI may take those jobs away! Be ready for more tough stuff ahead. And remember, never give up!

"Never cut a tree down in the wintertime. Never make a negative decision in the low time. Never make your most important decisions when you are in your worst moods. Wait. Be patient. The storm will pass. The spring will come."

— Robert H. Schuller, televangelist and motivational speaker

BONUS INSIGHTS

Leader Bonus Insight

After I'd been with a company for a few years, we ran into serious trouble. Our leader had just come from a senior executive meeting where the CEO asked everyone to keep the problems under wraps until a communication plan could be produced. But this leader managed all the people on the frontline, and he believed they needed as much advance notice as possible to prepare for negative press and upset customers. So, he asked everyone for their trust and told them he needed to look out for them — and the company at the same time. Our bank ended up failing and being sold over a year later. But this leader took us into his trust and actually inspired us to do everything we could do to help the company endure. Very few people quit, no one broke his trust — and most hung on with a desire to see the bank succeed. I think this EVP was a big reason why.

— Mark Crowley, author of *Lead from The Heart*

Leader Bonus Insight

Lead out loud! Start with you. Learn to learn and share your journey. If you want to learn something, try to teach it as soon as you can. If you are wrong, celebrate it and the people who helped you see it. Leading out loud is the number one way to grow, develop self-awareness and build the confidence you need to lead through ambiguity and duress.

— Michael Leckie, Founding Partner, Silverback Partners

CHAPTER 8

Caring Leadership Challenge

"We humans are emotional creatures; without that understanding, one cannot lead effectively."

— Germain St-Denis

Congratulations on reaching the last chapter and thank you for staying with me. By now, you understand my Architect of People First™ strategies and my Caring Leadership philosophy. These mindsets recognize the basic human needs and concerns that drive our emotions, decisions and actions. To be an effective leader of people and organizations, one must realize that the heart of leadership is the human connection. The rewards of doing so can be enormous.

You may have the potential to be a great leader and leave a legacy of positive impact on the people you serve. As you lead teams to achieve and be successful, you will presumably also be successful. However, herein lies the **Caring Leadership Challenge**:

1. Are you prepared to obtain job satisfaction and fulfillment *through* the success of your people?

2. Do you care enough about helping your people succeed to place their success and career development *ahead* of yours when needed?

Only you can truthfully answer these Challenge questions. You can seek guidance from your mentor, coach, leader and other key figures in your life. They may help you assess your skills and capabilities and your motivation to become a leader. Ultimately, your decision must come from you, from your rational brain, your gut and your heart. For many leaders, myself included, leadership is a passion and a commitment. Follow your passion and you will find your purpose.

"Have the courage to follow your heart and intuition. They somehow already know what you truly want to become."

— Steve Jobs, visionary businessman and
Co-Founder of Apple Inc.

If you accept the Caring Leadership Challenge, you are making a commitment to a higher standard of leadership. My hope is that this book has and will continue to help you. It is a tremendously gratifying experience to see your people succeed, knowing you had a role to play in making that happen.

Author and leadership guru John C. Maxwell says, "There is no success without sacrifice. Every person who has achieved any success in life has made sacrifices to do so." He adds, "The heart of leadership is putting others ahead of yourself. It's doing what is best for the team."

Yeah! You are taking the next steps to becoming a Caring Leader. Fortunately, there is a considerable amount of information at your disposal from your HR team, your leadership team, advisors, thought leaders and coaches. Various courses and related materials are also available.

Should you be interested in a collaborative approach and personalized coaching to benefit from my experience and elevate your leadership potential and that of your leadership team, there are several ways I can help, including my **Empowering Leaders *IN ACTION*** roundtable program. Please see my *About the Author* section. Connect on LinkedIn, visit my website, reach out when you're ready. I'd be happy to chat and learn about you and any challenges I may be able to help you with.

I close this last chapter of my book by first thanking you, dear reader. It is an absolute honour that you cared enough to read my book and to the very end, no less! With your support and the work of like-minded individuals, we *can* create a better workplace for everyone. It starts with each of us being a kind, caring person, and for some, becoming a Caring Leader. I thank you wholeheartedly!

Today, November 2nd, marks the day that my father died in an accident on his farm, already 33 years ago. I leave you with this quote as it applies as much to my Architect of People First™ strategies and my Caring Leadership philosophy as it did to my dad's life and legacy.

"The only thing that endures over time is the Law of the Farm. You must prepare the ground, plant the seed, cultivate, and water it if you expect to reap the harvest."

— Stephen R. Covey, author and renowned leadership authority

Closing Thoughts – What is Your Legacy Going to Be?

Simply put, legacy is what you leave behind, both tangible and intangible. You work hard in your career to earn and maintain a good reputation and to develop trusting relationships. What will people say when you are not around?

1. Did you serve, guide, coach, mentor, encourage, praise and develop others?

2. Did you make a difference and have a positive impact on people?

3. Are you or were you a caring person and a Caring Leader?

We can write our memoirs, even our own obituary. We can't write how people remember us. The story that is our legacy develops and is registered as we live our lives each day. As leaders, I believe our legacy should be based on how we helped others. **I would be thrilled if my legacy is that I helped people to be their best!**

"You reap what you sow."

ABOUT THE AUTHOR

Germain L. St-Denis believes that leadership is first and foremost about *helping people to be their best!*

Germain is an advocate for Caring Leadership, a style that he embodies and promotes through his extensive experience as a middle manager and executive leading teams in IT Consulting Services across North America. He realized early on that the way to impactful leadership is to care for people - those delivering the technology and those held to adopt it effectively. Germain is creator of Architect of People First™, a strategic approach to becoming a successful Caring Leader and achieving the right mindset that goes with it. His Caring Leadership style nurtures the best in people, resulting in cooperative, high-performing, loyal teams who excel at what they do.

His professional journey, marked by resilience and adaptability, emphasizes the importance of developing and empowering individuals and managers. Awarded for his outstanding achievements and having navigated significant industry challenges, including the aftermath of 9/11 and three acquisitions, Germain's leadership approach is deeply rooted in trust, empowerment and People First strategies.

After overcoming cancer, he embraced a reflective sabbatical before returning to the consulting sphere where he now focuses on fostering caring leadership and people-centred cultures. He shares his experience and insights through coaching services for individuals and groups with his **Empowering Leaders *IN ACTION*** roundtable program.

Recognized as a top thought leader in coaching and leadership, Germain invites collaborative engagements to amplify leadership potential and is available for connection through email, LinkedIn and his website.

germain@germainstdenis.ca
www.germainstdenis.ca
LinkedIn www.linkedin.com/in/germain-st-denis

ACKNOWLEDGEMENTS

Blessed! As I look back on my journey so far, I must say that I feel blessed. Blessed to have been born in our great country Canada and into a loving family with caring parents and supportive siblings. Blessed that God gave me a good brain, a positive outlook, the aptitude to learn and adapt, and the ability to relate to people.

I wish to acknowledge my family, first and foremost my parents who were kind and caring despite the heavy toil of raising ten children on a small farm. My mom was a strong yet kind-hearted woman, fun loving with a loud laugh, providing care, guidance and encouragement as we grew up. My dad was disciplined and dedicated, worked diligently on his farm, caring for animals, showing we kid the ropes and letting us learn from mistakes, and helping neighbours when he could. He was highly respected by all who knew him. Always authentic and no nonsense, my parents exemplified care, dedication, responsibility, accountability and resilience.

My older siblings, Adèle, Colette, Laurier, Hélène and Daniel who are living, and Denise, Yvon and Richard who are in heaven — paved the way for my younger brother Alain and me, at times providing guidance, at times gifts of affection. Colette is an accomplished author of several books, some masterfully sharing the story of our family and ancestry. Colette's books and Hélène's artistic design and formatting contributions to them were an inspiration for me to write my own. Through what seems like telepathy, Adèle came up with "Empowering People" for the title of my book at the same time I did, before I even discussed it with her. Uncanny, eh?

I appreciate the support provided by my ex-wife, Hélène, who cared for our children while I worked long hours and travelled for weeks at a time as a road warrior and international thought leader, as well as during the ups and downs brought on by my health issues.

To my son Louis, my daughter Christine and my grandchildren Camille, Nicolas, and Mélodie (Christine's), may this book and the real-life stories in it serve as a testament to kindness and caring. Through determination and resilience, we can accomplish our goals without impeding others, but rather by supporting them.

Through my work and my hobbies, I'm blessed to have met so many kind, smart and talented people who have helped and supported me along the way. I'm blessed with long lasting meaningful relationships and friendships. I am truly thankful that we were and, in many cases, continue to be part of each other's journey.

My heartful gratitude to those who believed in me and trusted me to join their team and to get things done and lead other people in a caring, humane manner – the way it should be. My most notable leaders and influencers start with Warren Parker and Pat Shea at Bell Canada, my very first job and one of my best experiences. At Canada Post, Gary Halpin, Peter McInenly, Doug Johnson, Dr. Ken Tucker, Hank Klassen and other executives supported my quest to make a significant impact in the development of international post and telecom electronic hybrid communications standards. That experience introduced me to several people from around the world, some becoming close friends. In fact, I'm in touch regularly with Alan Pugh in England.

At DMR Consulting Group, my heartfelt gratitude to Evan Diamond, John Simmons, Irene Sacharuk, Pierre Poitras, Tony Baldock, Paul Kent, John Thorp and executives at head office in Montreal. This was one of the best periods in my career and the best place to work at the time. Too many friends to list.

In the new millennium, thanks to Geoff Ribek, Cliff Booth, Stephen Mahoney, Markus Reschberger and the entire sales team at BEA Systems for their collaboration and support as my team achieved tremendous success. At Oracle Consulting, Steve Matola, Steve Verba (RIP), Teresa Short, Marc Horowitz, Kerry Tarr, Mohan Natarajan and members of the sales team. At Ceridian, Beth Carroll, Shelly Sharp, Lori Collins, Ann Phillips and Christine Parent.

Since I left the corporate world, there have been several key individuals who have influenced and supported me in my journey as a management consultant and interim leader. I'm blessed with many social media followers on LinkedIn who contribute valuable content and support my activity. I'd like to acknowledge key individuals who have become close collaborators and friends:

— Peter Goral, Social Media Strategist at ArtEnvy Inc. (Marketing Solutions) A master in the art of meaningful human connection, a model Servant Leader, impactful with his clients, caring and willing to do whatever it takes to help others be successful. Peter has helped me more times than I can remember, including creating my social media brand and presence, and continues to share insights and promote my work. Cheers and thank you, Peter!

— Patrick McKenna, an internationally recognized author, lecturer, strategist and seasoned advisor to the leaders of premier professional service firms, yet also my occasional mentor and sounding board. Patrick has a unique way of approaching and questioning things, in the process getting us to re-think what we are trying to achieve and how we're going about it. This book has been tremendously enriched by Patrick's suggestions, support, guidance and example over the past 4-5 years. Sincere thanks for your exemplary leadership and wisdom, Patrick!

— Mark Crowley put himself out there by leading with care, empathy and compassion, and captured the magic in his book *Lead From The Heart*, initiating a movement that I stand firmly behind. My sincere heartfelt thanks, Mark, for your work and for graciously writing a masterpiece Foreword for my book!

— Michael Leckie, thank you for the nuggets of wisdom that you share, for your leadership in placing people front and centre in digital transformations, and for your ongoing support.

A sincere thank you to key women in leadership who trusted and supported me, recognized and championed my efforts. I appreciate our ongoing relationships and friendships: Irene Sacharuk (DMR), Teresa Short (Oracle), Beth Carroll (Ceridian), Cecilia Carbonelli (an executive client).

There are many others, yet I can't name everyone. You know who you are. Rest assured that not being mentioned does not take anything away from the contributions you have made to my career and my life.

A special thank you to all authors, influencers, leaders, former colleagues and team members who answered my questionnaire and contributed meaningful insights to this book, adding tremendous value and amplifying the importance of Caring Leadership. I'm also very grateful to all those who graciously agreed to pre-read my book PDF and provide their feedback and valued endorsement.

My heartfelt and utmost gratitude to my wife, Janice McNally, who helped me face surgeries and cancer treatment, now doing double duty as a communications professional and editor of my book. Plowing through several iterations and corrections have not only made my book a better read but also vastly improved the clarity of my Caring Leadership message to you, my readers.

Perhaps the most important of all, a HUGE thank you to everyone who has ever been a member of my staff, either as individual contributors or managers — I appreciate you all! My team has always been my secret weapon. Without a team's full support and cooperation, a leader can never be as effective and impactful. Caring Leadership and the human connection make all the difference!

REFERENCES

Foreword

Lead from the Heart: Transformational Leadership For The 21st Century
Mark C. Crowley (2022 and 2011 editions)

Introduction

What is Servant Leadership?
The Greenleaf Center for Servant Leadership

Chapter 1

First Among Equals – How to Manage a Group of Professionals
Patrick J. McKenna and David H. Maister, 2005

The Unlock Moment podcast with Dr Gary Crotaz, PhD
Episode 76 – "Germain St-Denis: Leadership Is Helping People To Be Their Best"

"Do you want to retain top talent? Be a better leader."
McKinsey Themes, April 2022

Chapter 2

Primal Leadership – Realizing the Power of Emotional Intelligence
Daniel Goleman, Richard Boyatzis, Annie McKee, 2002

SERVANT LEADERSHIP A Minute with John Maxwell
YouTube

Chapter 3
"The Leader as Coach"
Harvard Business Review Magazine, November–December 2019

"To Improve Your Performance as a Leader, Seek Feedback"
Debra Roberts, *Inc.com, July 2022*

Chapter 4
"Do You Lead with Your Head, Your Heart or Your Hands?"
EHS Today, June 2013

The Driving Force, Extraordinary Results with Ordinary People
Peter W. Schutz, Former CEO of Porsche AG, 2005

"Connect, Then Lead"
Amy J.C. Cuddy, Matthew Kohut and John Neffinger
Harvard Business Review Magazine, July 2013

Quiet: The Power of Introverts in a World That Can't Stop Talking
Susan Cain, 2012

"Gone for now, or gone for good? How to play the new talent game and win back workers"
McKinsey Quarterly, March 2022

Chapter 5
"Can 5 Generations Coexist in The Workplace"
Forbes, March 2023

"Meet the Perennials"
Gina Pell, *The WHAT List*, Oct 2016

The Perennials, The Megatrends Creating
A Postgenerational Society
Mauro F. Guillén, 2023

The 100-Year Life: Living and Working in an Age of Longevity
Lynda Gratton and Andrew J. Scott, 2017

"Now that many of us will live to 100, this is what our careers will look like"
Kristen Sieffert, *Fast Company*, Nov 2022

"Why People Are Quitting Their Jobs"
Martin Armstrong, *Statista,* Jul 2022

Inside Out Empathy: Explore the Underestimated Superpower Essential for Building, Developing, And Inspiring a Rock-Solid Team
Erin Thorp, 2017

Leadership Strategies for the Hybrid Workforce: Best Practices for Fostering Employee Safety and Significance
Matthew Ohlson, Lakshmi Goel, IGI Global, 2022
Chapter 7: *"Employees Feeling Significant in a Hybrid Workforce"* by Douglas J. Dawson

The Why of Work
Dave Ulrich and Wendy Ulrich, 2010

Human Capability and the Future of Work
Dave Ulrich, YouTube, Nov 2022

Chapter 6

"HP CEO Enrique Lores: The world has an unhealthy relationship with work"
Fast Company, Oct 2023

"Farmers CEO Reverses Course to Require Hybrid Work Schedule for Employees"
Insurance Journal, June 2023

"The non-linear workdays changing the shape of productivity"
BBC Worklife, Oct 2022

Evolve: The Path to Trauma-Informed Leadership
Carolyn Swora, 2023

The Heart of Transformation: Build the Human Capabilities that Change Organizations for Good
Michael J. Leckie, 2021

Chapter 7

Life Is Hard: How Philosophy Can Help Us Find Our Way
Kieran Setiya, 2022

Printed in Great Britain
by Amazon

51275348R00089